WHO SAYS
YOU
CAN'T?

D1265099

KINGSLEY
FLETCHER

Charisma
HOUSE
A STRANG COMPANY

Most STRANG COMMUNICATIONS/CHARISMA HOUSE/CHRISTIAN LIFE/ EXCEL BOOKS/FRONTLINE/REALMS/SILOAM products are available at special quantity discounts for bulk purchase for sales promotions, premiums, fundraising, and educational needs. For details, write Strang Communications Book Group, 600 Rinehart Road, Lake Mary, Florida 32746, or telephone (407) 333-0600.

WHO SAYS YOU CAN'T? by Kingsley Fletcher (HRM, King Adamtey I)
Published by Charisma House
A Strang Company
600 Rinehart Road
Lake Mary, Florida 32746
www.strangdirect.com

Unless otherwise noted, all Scripture quotations are from the Holy Bible, New International Version of the Bible. Copyright © 1973, 1978, 1984, International Bible Society. Used by permission.

Scripture quotations marked NKJV are from the New King James Version of the Bible. Copyright © 1979, 1980, 1982 by Thomas Nelson, Inc., publishers. Used by permission.

Scripture quotations marked KJV are from the King James Version of the Bible.

Design Director: Bill Johnson
Cover design by studiogearbox.com

Library of Congress Cataloging-in-Publication Data:
Fletcher, Kingsley A.
  Who says you can't? / Kingsley Fletcher. -- 1st ed.
      p. cm.
  ISBN 978-1-59979-463-1
  1. Success--Religious aspects--Christianity. 2. Attitude (Psychology)-
-Religious aspects--Christianity. 3. Thought and thinking--Religious
aspects--Christianity. 4. Optimism. 5. Negativism. I. Title.
  BV4598.3.F54 2009
  158--dc22
                                        2008040431

First Edition

09 10 11 12 13 — 987654321
Printed in the United States of America

To all those who have had a vision or goal that someone has attempted to steal, divert, or destroy, this book is for you! May it bring you the freedom to achieve the dreams that others call impossible! If God didn't say it, then it is just an opinion!

[CONTENTS]

[PREFACE]

WHO SAYS YOU CAN'T? provides powerful insight and direction on how to accomplish your purpose in life and fulfill your dreams. *Who Says You Can't?* is a road map to achieving success through positive thoughts, positive words, and surrounding yourself with positive people. This book will teach you how to seek out and discover the divine purpose, plan, and destiny for your life and how to achieve a rich and successful life filled with potential and possibilities. You will come away empowered, energized, inspired, and motivated to pursue your dreams and accomplish your goals.

This book will teach you how to destroy the influences of negativity, defeat, and despair, which have been designed to rob you of your destiny. You will learn how to toss out the garbage and unnecessary baggage in your life and to live triumphantly through the miracles of grace, favor, and predestined purpose. It speaks to the heart of everyone who has had a dream that was shattered or questioned by someone held as an authority figure. When the negativity expressed by these *dream stoppers* influences our lives and causes us to put our dreams on hold, our potential is lost.

Who Says You Can't? encourages you to break the chains of stigma placed upon you, to rise above average and become the champion of your life's dream. *You* hold the keys to your own destiny! No one can limit your potential by his or her words, attitudes, or actions. If *GOD* didn't say you couldn't do it—*YOU CAN!* You *will* achieve all that you have in your heart to do. You do not need to fear the limitations others have tried to place on you. You *are* victorious, and your potential is unlimited!

The purpose of this book is to enlighten and empower you to accept your potential in all spheres of life and to stretch your boundaries to reach them. I will give you practical examples from the lives of many successful people from many areas of influence, people who have overcome various forms of challenges and even defeat, only to rise to the top level of success in their fields.

As you discover how others have utilized the power of positive words, the power of positive thoughts, and the power of positive people to effect change in their spheres of influence, you will gain insight on the very ways you can use these forces in your own life. You will come away stronger and more determined than ever that the delays you face en route to your goals will help you to achieve them in a more powerful way!

Who Says You Can't? takes away all the man-made barriers preventing you from reaching your potential and achieving your dreams. This book is a fresh and encouraging look at the road to success!

[ACKNOWLEDGMENTS]

FIRST OF ALL, I wish to acknowledge the Source of my life, whose divine love, wisdom, and protection have brought me thus far and who continues to influence all that I do.

This book would not be possible without the expertise of a great team who worked tirelessly to bring my vision to fruition. Special thanks to:

My immediate family—for your ongoing support and encouragement. I love you all very much.

Valerie K. Fields—for your exceptional editorial assistance. You are excellent at what you do, and your contributions to this book were invaluable.

Paula Diley—for managing this project from beginning to end. Thanks a million for a job well done.

Pamela Evans, Johnnie McGill, Marcus Plating, and the entire staff and members of LCC of Research Triangle Park—for being the first recipients of these principles.

The Se (Shai) people in Ghana and the Diaspora—you are truly the motivating factor for many things that I do.

Vickie and Malcolm Au; Phil Chien; Carl and Jeannie Chien; Fred and Linda Ma; Margaret, Cher, Susan, and family; and Frank and Lisa Santora—for all your faithful support.

Stephen Strang and the Charisma House family—for your contributions and expertise.

1

WHO SAYS YOU CAN'T?

I F YOU HAVE EVER had a dream but have been too afraid to pursue it, this book is for you. If you have ever felt you were living beneath your purpose but don't know how to discover it, this book is for you. If you have ever looked closely at your life and realized you are not living or achieving the divine plan for your life—again, this book is for you.

Every person has a divine plan, purpose, and destiny that each of us is obligated to fulfill. We must confront mental, physical, spiritual, financial, and emotional limitations and setbacks in order to overcome trauma and defeat and achieve success. If you are ready to nullify the existence of impossibility in your life, then this book is for you.

At some time, every person on this earth has questioned his or her life's purpose or his or her place in this world. It is instinctively human to doubt or question your place in this world. Rest assured that the answers are within your reach. Tapping into the well of wisdom, knowledge, and guidance for your life is simply a matter of arriving at the right fountain of resources. It is often a matter of listening to what life has to say and observing the signs that life gives to direct you to the optimal path toward the greater good of mankind. For some, that discovery is an instantaneous revelation of truth; for others, it's a lifelong journey or quest for answers.

In many instances, people have identified their purpose, discovered life's plan, and glimpsed their destiny, but yet missed the mark and fallen short of their goals—simply because someone told them, "You can't."

Those two small but powerful words have been responsible for more abandoned dreams, missed opportunities, and premature failures in life than anyone can imagine. But the two words *you can* are just as powerful and potent as the words *you can't.*

Many people have convictions, but most of us are not willing to die for our convictions. We have a cause, but we aren't truly committed to it. Having the ability to assert, "I can," requires remaining determined in spite of any challenges or difficulties that come your way. Saying "I can" takes courage, determination, and willpower. You must be willing to count the costs, to take calculated risks, to do something you've never done before, and to go places you've never gone before. Asserting "I can" means being willing to walk out your hopes and aspirations until they become actions and realizations. *I can* means taking action. It meant that *you can't* is no longer acceptable—those two words no longer keep you from simply believing that *you can!*

IF GOD DIDN'T SAY IT, THEN IT'S ONLY SOMEONE ELSE'S OPINION!

Who says you can't accomplish your goals? Who says you can't be successful? Who says you can't lose weight? Who says you'll never escape your past? Who says you'll never amount to anything? Who says you don't deserve to be happy? Who says your marriage won't last? Who says your children can't have fulfilling lives? Who says you can't enjoy freedom from various types of addictions? Who says you can't start a business? Who says you can't finish school? Who says you'll always be broke? Who says you'll never learn how to forgive? Who says you'll never love again? Who says you'll never own a home? Who says you'll never be anything but a failure? Who says there's no hope for you?

WHO SAYS YOU CAN'T?

Let's agree in the beginning that there is one sure and final authority in our lives, and He is God. If you can initially accept and agree that there is a power greater than your circumstances, experiences, perceptions, and surroundings, then you can grasp that there is a divine plan for your life and a divine authority in place to help you accomplish it.

By whose authority have you been making decisions for your life? Are you still basing the outcome of your life on the words of someone who didn't believe in you? Are you still being hindered by the negative influences of your childhood? Are the broken dreams of your past depleting the potential for your future?

No one enters this world void of a purpose, plan, and destiny that has been assigned since the beginning of time. Our objective is to discover that individual and unique plan and then fulfill the potential of the life we've been assigned. Without question, there will be difficulties, challenges, and obstacles that arise to distract and discourage us from discovering our purpose, but we've been given a divine promise of success, and it is our responsibility to accept nothing less than overwhelming victory. God has given each of us an Instruction Manual that tells us that through faith, positive affirmation, and perseverance we can do *all* things. That statement has the ability to alter the structure of your future and establish the foundation of your faith. Are you willing to believe that it is possible to live life without limits? Are you willing to believe that the best is yet to come? Are you willing to believe that you can? Who says you can't?

We live in a world of possibilities—a "can-be," "can-do" society where nothing is impossible. You are a person with a purpose, which means that there is a specific assignment or life task that you've been given and must fulfill before you exit this realm. You are a person with a plan, which means there is a right way and there is a wrong way to accomplish your life goals. The plan for your life may lead you to different people, places, and situations than you ever imagined possible, but ultimately it leads to your predestined purpose in life. You are a person with a destiny. Nothing happens by chance, but rather by circumstance. You alone are responsible for reacting and responding to the circumstances in your life.

As people with a purpose, plan, and destiny, we cannot afford to use confusion, chaos, and difficult circumstances as excuses for failure. You are a person with a purpose, a plan, and a destiny, and you can no longer accept *you can't*. You must simply believe that *you can*. If you can conceive it and believe it, then there's no reason you can't achieve it. The time has arrived to take action and refuse to take *no* for an answer.

Stop for a moment and think about the people in your life who have said, "You can't." Perhaps it was a parent, a teacher, a friend, or even a spouse. Maybe it was a neighbor, a stranger, a relative, or an enemy. Countless individuals have allowed themselves to stagnate in life and settle for less because some other person did not believe in their ability.

This book was written to help break the limitations off your life and help change your thinking about yourself and what you can do in your future.

My Own *You Can't* Challenges

I vividly remember being told "You can't" when I was a child. If I had listened to what was said, I wouldn't be where I am today. When I was a boy, I was injured by a poisonous arrow shot through my right eye—leaving me poisoned, blind, and in a coma. I recall my parents telling the story from the perspective of the doctor, who told them I would never come out of the coma and that I was going to die. I was in a coma for three months. When I finally came out of it, the doctor said that because of the poison in my body, I would not live past my next birthday. Well, as you know, I'm still here, and I've lived well past that prediction. While the doctors were saying, "He can't live," I knew there was a purpose, plan, and destiny for my life that I had to fulfill.

I spent an entire year in the hospital and three of those months in a coma. I wasn't expected to live; I was expected to die. But expectation and realization are not the same. If you have a plan, purpose, and destiny that require you to live and make a positive difference in the world, then that's what has to happen. On nine different occasions the doctors who dealt with my type of injury predicted that I would not live. Yet I'm still here because the words and opinions of others do not have the final authority in my life.

When I regained consciousness and began the road to recovery, I went through life just like anyone else. But because of the negative things that had been spoken over me, I now had unnecessary limitations imposed on my life. I decided that I would not think about what I could not do; I simply focused on what I could do, what I was purposed to do, and what I had to do. Everything begins with a choice. I chose to ignore the negative words that people said. I chose to ignore the negative prognosis for my health. I chose to ignore the prediction of failure and defeat. I accepted the fact that my life had a plan. I accepted the fact that my life had a purpose. I accepted the fact that if I was going to achieve my destiny, I had to be alive to do it. I chose to live my life according to its divine purpose. I simply chose to accentuate the positive and eliminate the negative and think in terms of success rather than failure.

> ONCE YOU ARE DEFEATED IN YOUR MIND, YOU WILL BE DEFEATED IN YOUR LIFE.

In other words, I had to retrain my mind to think right and then act right—based on my thinking. Once you are defeated in your mind, you will be defeated in your life. Wrong thinking leads to wrong actions, so it's very important to be surrounded by the right thoughts and ideas.

I believe most of us have been through similar scenarios in life. There are things you were told you couldn't do, and as a result, you didn't even try. Many things have been told to us, and if we only believe what we hear from people instead of what we know is true, we will never accomplish our ultimate purpose in life.

I was born in Ghana, West Africa. Within the African culture, respect and honor are given to the elderly and whatever they say. There were a lot of people who told me that I couldn't become what I wanted to be. For example, I always knew I had a mission to inspire hope in the world and to help humanity. I've always believed that part of my calling was to be a humanitarian and an inspirational leader, to lead people and to teach others how to lead. At the time, though, no one had ever heard of an African missionary, so I wasn't encouraged to come here to the West. But in my heart, I knew it was what I was supposed to do.

Over the years, I've worked as a missionary, an author, and a motivational speaker in Africa, Europe, Asia, and the United States. Throughout the years, I've directed countless people to discover their destiny and begin down the path of purpose for their lives. It has been one of my greatest joys to help restore families by sharing inspiring and uplifting words and encouraging individuals to rediscover their faith and their inherent ability to believe that they can overcome life's challenges and strengthen their family ties.

INSPIRING HOPE

I want to give people hope. I want people to believe that life has good things in store for them, and I want people to know that it is neither necessary nor acceptable to settle for less than the best that life has to offer. I want people to know that time can heal all wounds. I want people to know that love overcomes pain. I want people to know that forgiveness is a part of love and that we all need to give and receive both.

My travels from Africa to Europe as a young man allowed me to see a lot of suffering and despair. So my desire has always been to serve others and inspire them to a better way of life.

Over the years I've learned several truths. And one of them is that "hurting people hurt people." It became evident that part of my purpose in life was to help people to stop hurting and as a result, to stop hurting others. I've witnessed many marriages and families breaking up because one spouse is hurting, and, in turn, that person hurts his or her mate and children. I realized that the world has been deceived into thinking that 50 percent or more of all marriages ultimately must end in divorce, or that a significant number of young people will become rebellious and destructive because of their dysfunctional families. Statistics and theories are just numbers and words. They do not have any authority on what can or cannot happen in our lives. If marriage and family are important to you and are part of the plan, purpose, and destiny for your life, then you can have a happy family—who says you can't?

I believe in the power of prayer and meditation, and I encourage everyone I encounter to do the same. I also believe that everything in our life works together for the greatest good of all. I accept that bad things happen in our lives—often to make us stronger or more aware of our place and purpose in the world. I know that trials serve to strengthen us, and that disappointment and heartache ground us and force us to rely on our faith. Without a doubt, I know that everything we need to fulfill the divine plan, purpose, and destiny for our lives is inherently a part of who we are. It is simply our duty to discover that aspect of ourselves and refuse to accept man-made limitations on our abilities. Everything that man said I could not do, I'm doing! So, as I reflect on these things, I say, "Now, why, then, would I listen to human limitations?" People may try to put limitations on you based on tradition, the past, or their own experiences, but don't let them do it. Only you and your divine destiny can define the boundaries and limits of your life.

Learn the Concept of Favor

I want to introduce you to a concept that you probably don't hear or think about very often. It's the idea of *favor*. Did you ever have a favorite teacher, a favorite friend, or a favorite pet? Most likely you treated your *favorite* a little better than the rest. Favor is a principle that works through the spiritual law of reciprocity. In other words, what goes around comes around. Favor with others can be gained through hard work, honesty, humility, sensitivity, and selflessness. In and of itself, favor is its own reward for making positive contributions into the lives of others. But in most instances, favor is simply granted without any prerequisite. You don't always need a reason for something to be your favorite; it just is. Similar to luck—but more reliable—favor can elevate you far beyond where money, power, or influence can.

If someone shows you favor, you don't have to do anything to acquire it. Along the way on life's journey, giving favor to others through charity, love, sacrifice, and forgiveness is the beginning of walking the right path toward your destiny and part of the never-ending process of achieving your purpose.

Life is an evolution, and the moment you stop changing, growing, and evolving, you essentially identify the place where you want to die. Life is filled with change, which requires flexibility and adaptation. The plan and purpose for your life work together to guide you toward your ultimate destiny. We must decide to live life to the fullest lest we die prematurely and shortchange the world of our contributions.

One of the greatest lessons that life has to offer is that nothing is free. The price we pay for success is usually comprised of hard work, determination, commitment, and perseverance. The negative things in your life that have hindered your progress didn't happen overnight. They took time, energy, and resources, so consequently, the things that you must implement to be successful will also take time, energy, and resources. There are no overnight miracles or quick fixes. There is only resolve and belief in the power of *I can* and an unshakable faith in the pursuit of your God-given purpose.

> WE MUST WATER AND NURTURE THE WORDS THAT PLANT POSITIVE MESSAGES, AND WE MUST EDIT AND DISCARD THE WORDS THAT SEED NEGATIVE AND DESTRUCTIVE MESSAGES.

THE POWER OF WORDS—AND THOUGHTS

What are you saying about your life? Words have power, and when you speak, ultimately you empower your words to materialize. Each of us has the ability to speak curses or blessings in our lives. Consider the idea that your words are building blocks for the foundation of your life. Speaking positive and encouraging words manifests positive and encouraging results, ultimately building self-esteem, confidence, and purpose. Negative and demeaning words not only weaken that foundation but also tear down the stable elements of your life already in place. A few harsh words spoken at an early age can follow, haunt, and hinder an individual for a lifetime. Enough negativity in someone's life becomes an outright assault against productivity, prosperity, and success. That's why it's important to commit to speaking and entertaining uplifting conversations. In some sense, the foundation of your life may depend on it.

We must be very careful of the thoughts and ideas we allow to enter our minds. We are often influenced by the day-to-day voices from family and friends, the voices of our enemies, the voice of our own conscious and selfish desires, and the voices from our past. Words are like seeds that are planted in our subconscious to take root. So we must be selective of the words that we allow others to implant in our minds. We must water and nurture the words that plant positive messages, and we must edit and discard the words that seed negative and destructive messages.

The formulation of any plan—good or bad, positive or

negative—begins in your mind. So, if someone wants to destroy your confidence, discourage you, or frustrate you, they need only to plant a seed of negativity in your mind. If a negative seed is planted in fertile ground, where it is watered and fed, it will continue to grow. And if it grows long enough, the roots will grow deeper, and it will be planted so deeply that it will become very difficult to uproot.

If you ever meet an adult who has low self-esteem and low self-confidence, and who only thinks the worst of himself or herself, I guarantee that if you could look back into that person's life, you'd find a little child who was discouraged, mistreated, or undervalued. The seeds that were planted in that person's childhood were fertilized with anger instead of love, intolerance instead of patience, abuse instead of compassion, and discouragement instead of encouragement.

Whatever you hear, good or bad, will have an impact on you. So what have you been accused of over the years that would make you believe you can't be successful? What lies have been told to you that say you can't live a wonderful and fulfilling life? What untruths have been planted in your mind about your ability to accomplish great things? How many times have you been accused, criticized, or condemned? How many times have you been misjudged or overlooked? Who's been talking to you, and to whom have you been listening? What gossip has been used to destroy your life? How long will others try to hold your past against you? Who said you have to keep listening? Who said you can't be free? If God didn't say it, then it's only someone else's opinion!

You were created with a purpose and a plan in mind. When you look in the mirror, you must see yourself as you were created to be, not as you are right now or as you were back then. When you endeavor to begin a new task, a new life, or a new future, you must begin with the end in mind. You must start knowing that you are going to finish. You must act as if the only option you have is overwhelming success. You must live as if there are no limitations on your life and believe as if you cannot fail.

WE MUST LEARN TO SEE OURSELVES FROM A PURPOSE POINT OF VIEW.

In many instances throughout history, people's names were changed when it was time for them to fulfill their destiny. What names have you been called? Maybe it's time to change your name—or at least the name to which you answer. It's time to answer to your purpose—not your past—and to walk into your divine destiny.

Whether we're discussing biblical characters, historical figures, or our own current situations, the fact still remains that our lives have a divine purpose that is inseparable from who we are and what we've been called to accomplish in life. Consider the story of Gideon in the Book of Judges, chapter 6. The children of Israel, whom God had protected, delivered, and blessed, now broke their covenant with Him, turned their backs on God, forsook Him, and worshiped idols. Because of their sin,

God removed His divine protection and abundant supply from heaven and turned them over to the hands of their enemies, the Midianites and the Amalekites. When they repented and cried out, He sent them an angel with a message that He would once again deliver them.

The angel came and sat under a nearby oak tree where Gideon was threshing wheat to hide from his enemies. "When the angel of the LORD appeared to Gideon, he said, 'The LORD is with you, mighty warrior'" (Judg. 6:12). In spite of the fact that Gideon was hiding, fearing destruction by his enemies, and rehearsing the many defeats and humiliation he and his men had suffered at the hands of the Midianites and the Amalekites, the angel came calling Gideon by what he was destined to be—*a mighty man of valor.*

Gideon was scared, running for his life, and hiding from his perceived enemies. Interestingly, God did not approach him and say, "Hey, coward, let Me help you out of this situation again." Rather, God came to him and said something about him that he did not even believe about himself. God said to him through the angel, "Hey warrior…conqueror…mighty man of valor…I am with you!" God said these words to him, but Gideon didn't believe them. As a matter of fact, he came up with several excuses for why it couldn't be so. Isn't it interesting how even when God tries to deliver or rescue us from our undesirable past and set us free, we still come up with excuses to remain in bondage? For so long we've fed our spirits with negative things and negative words that we've started to believe them. Then when God calls us to something higher—something greater—we don't even recognize whom He's talking to.

Similarly, if a person doesn't have confidence and feel good about himself, no matter what positive things you tell him, he won't really believe them. Why? Because he has listened to negative thoughts and words for so long that those seeds have grown, taken root, and sprouted branches.

For example, if you compliment someone by saying that person looks nice, the person may respond negatively and put himself or herself down. Instead of responding to your words by saying, "Thank you. I've been working out at the gym," or "What a nice thing to say. I just bought this outfit," he or she may say something like, "Oh, no, I don't—I look terrible," or "You don't really mean that. You know I can't do anything with my hair." What could have been a genuine and pleasant conversation meant to compliment someone and boost confidence has now turned into a self-destructive analysis of all the negative things that person thinks or may have heard.

It's the same with life. Often when people grow up in an environment where they have been put down and berated with so many negative things about themselves, they tend to judge their outlook on life by their present circumstances, therefore robbing themselves of their future potential.

We must learn to see ourselves from a purpose point of view. In that regard, the focus is not so much about our past—*where we came from, what we used to do, what we used to be*—but on our potential—*who we are and where we're going*. Only your enemies are interested in your past, because misery loves company! Destiny and purpose are future focused. We need to recognize our potential and also our ability to achieve whatever we desire in life.

Someone once said, "Show me your friends, and I'll show you your future." All the old proverbs and wise sayings we hear have some truth to them; for example: If you lie down with dogs, you will get up with fleas. Water rises to its own level. Birds of a feather flock together, and so on.

We should all take a moment to examine the messages that our eyes, ears, and minds are receiving. What kind of information are you allowing to enter your mind? Whose voice are you listening to? What kind of information influences your life and your family? What words do you speak to yourself and your family in the morning to encourage them? What attitudes are you allowing to thrive and survive in your household? What things from the past are you still holding on to that are limiting your potential? What are you waiting for? If your Creator said you can, who says you can't?

The power of positive words

We have the innate ability to speak situations into existence. The Instruction Manual for our life tells us that the power of life and death is in the tongue (Prov. 18:21). We know that as faithful believers, when we pray and believe that what God says will happen, it will happen. That means it is literally possible to speak your desired circumstances into existence. We have the creative ability to speak to our circumstances and create change.

In the beginning, the *rhema* word—or spoken word—was used to initiate the creation of the universe. At first there was nothing, then the power of words became evident, and consequently there was something.

Many of us learned this lesson in Sunday school or kindergarten class. We simply learned and believed that "God said" and it happened. So the ability to speak things into existence is very real and very much a part of the divine inheritance we receive as powerful and creative beings. Understand this: when you speak powerful words and decree something, you issue an official statement or decision. Once you declare or decree something about your life, it shall be established—or set in motion—to manifest itself to you.

The power of positive thoughts

Positive thoughts can propel us into unimaginable success and accomplishments. Negative thoughts can restrict our growth and put severe limitations on our lives. "For as he thinks in his heart, so is he" (Prov. 23:7, NKJV). There is a popular book titled *Think and Grow Rich*.[1] The book doesn't instruct readers to "work harder and grow rich," or to "win the lottery and grow rich." It simply instructs us to change our thoughts and our thinking process, and the results can be increased wealth and riches. How you think about yourself and your potential will be the basis of what you can expect to happen. Your thoughts regarding a situation naturally set up an expectation for results. If you think you can win, you can. If you think you're doomed to fail, you are. The power of your thoughts has the ability to manifest into reality.

The power of positive people

Show me your friends, and I'll show you your future. Peer pressure among teenagers is one of the best examples I can think of to demonstrate the power of positive and negative influences. Around the world, peer pressure has been named as the culprit for the increases in teenage pregnancy, drug and alcohol abuse, and smoking for adolescents and teenagers. It's no wonder we don't want our children associating with the "wrong crowd." The negative attitudes and behaviors that result from the wrong group of friends can easily influence their behavior and negate their positive actions. Have you ever noticed how one negative encounter can impact your whole mind-set? If one person doesn't like your idea, or if one person disagrees with your suggestion, that one thought can extinguish your excitement or diffuse your drive to move forward. If you want to lose weight, stop smoking, start exercising, become a better spouse, read more, save money, or eat more healthily, make sure you surround yourself with positive people who speak positive words to encourage you.

Sometimes it is difficult for us to believe that we can be successful when our past and our current circumstances seem contrary to the slightest possibility of success. It's difficult to grasp a sunny and bright future when the bills are due, the bank account is empty, and we are heavily in debt. It's hard to believe that you're going to impact the world when your business fails...again. It's hard to be encouraged when the car gets repossessed and you're sitting home in the dark because the lights have been turned off.

But something we must always remember is that no condition is permanent, and defeat will only stay with us if we hang on to it. Let me say that again: *no condition is permanent, and defeat will only stay with us if we hang on to it!*

OVERCOMING TRIALS AND ADVERSITY

Let's look at Old Testament, New Testament, and modern-day examples of overcoming trials and adversity.

IT IS INSTINCTIVELY HUMAN TO DOUBT OR QUESTION YOUR PLACE IN THIS WORLD. REST ASSURED THAT THE ANSWERS ARE WITHIN YOUR REACH.

God gave Abraham and Sarah a promise: they would conceive a child of their own to leave as an inheritance. Consider their circumstances: Abraham was a hundred years old, and his wife, Sarah, was ninety. Having a child was a physical impossibility according to their knowledge and *facts* about childbearing. They were both well past the years of virility and fertility and had no hopes of returning to them. "Surely, God must have been mistaken," Sarah laughed. (See Genesis 18:12.) But God is not concerned about physical, mental, or emotional limitations from the past. God is only concerned with His Word and His truth. And once He speaks it, it must come to pass.

20

A year later, Sarah and Abraham were blessed with a son— Isaac. In spite of what appeared to be a hopeless situation, God was able to step in and bless them. No matter how bleak a situation may seem or how hopeless it appears, no condition is permanent.

People all over the world acknowledge Jesus Christ as one of the most significant, powerful, and influential leaders of all time. The record-breaking success of Mel Gibson's movie *The Passion of the Christ* is a testament to the world's fascination with His life. In the film, the Bible, and commentary of countless authors, we acknowledge and accept that Jesus lived a sinless and blameless life here on Earth. He dwelt here to fulfill His divine purpose to redeem mankind back to God by sacrificing His life on the cross at Calvary. Imagine the pain, agony, frustration, and disappointment He must have felt by taking on the consequences and punishment for sins He never committed. Imagine the heartbreak He must have felt when His beloved Father turned away and forsook Him. Consider the anguish He experienced, knowing that even though He gave His life, countless individuals would still despise Him. And yet, He did it anyway because it was the plan, purpose, and destiny for His life. What an amazing testimony to the power of unconditional love and the unwavering commitment to purpose and destiny.

Nelson Mandela is a modern-day hero, a living legend who committed his life's work to condemning the racial injustices of apartheid in South Africa. In 1964, during his trial for sabotage against the South African government, Mandela said:

I have cherished the ideal of a democratic and free
society in which all persons live together in harmony
and with equal opportunities. It is an ideal which I
hope to live for and achieve. But, if need be, it is an
ideal for which I am prepared to die.[2]

Mandela was convicted and imprisoned, sacrificing his
freedom for his beliefs and convictions. He displayed remarkable strength and tenacity under very trying and difficult
circumstances. His selfless acts of courage and altruism serve as
an exemplary model for others to follow. In 1990, Mandela was
released from prison, and four years later, he was elected as the
first black president of South Africa.

Another great hero of modern times is Mahatma Gandhi, an
individual who dedicated his life to demonstrating and perpetu-
ating the philosophy of nonviolence. Born on October 2, 1869,
Mohandas Karamchand Gandhi waged a nonviolent war against
oppression for his fellow countrymen. He was eventually given
the name "Mahatma," which means "great soul."

As a young man, Gandhi traveled to England to study law
and was admitted to the bar. It was during his stay in South
Africa that he first experienced racial discrimination and took
up the mantle to fight for the oppressed. There he began his
fight to end prejudice and achieve equality for people of all races.
During this time he began to change, studying the Bhagavad
Gita, the Christian Bible, and the writings of Thoreau, Ruskin,
and Tolstoy. He decided to forgo wealth and fineries and focus
instead on self-improvement. Gandhi used protest marches,

letters, articles, community meetings, and boycotts to actively resist. These protests often led to his arrest.

After twenty-one years in South Africa, Gandhi returned to India to fight for Indian independence from Great Britain. In addition to the methods he used in South Africa, Gandhi would add fasting and prayer to his expression of nonviolent protest. Perhaps he is most revered for his "fasts unto death" (hunger strikes), which often pressured government officials to comply with the wishes of the people. Gandhi spent many terms in jail as a result of his defiance against an unfair and unbalanced government and judicial system. Gandhi was assassinated in January 1948 on his way to evening prayers. His legacy includes many books, writings, and an enduring teaching that passive resistance—as opposed to violence—is a more powerful weapon, and that the enduring and indomitable spirit of one man with a purpose can ultimately overcome and achieve a greater good for all mankind.[3]

> YOU CAN BREAK ANY LIMITATION THAT HAS BEEN SET IN YOUR LIFE——SOCIETAL, CULTURAL, EMOTIONAL, EDUCATIONAL, ENVIRONMENTAL, OR ECONOMIC.

There are few more powerful examples and demonstrations of trials and adversity. It is from these examples that we draw faith, strength, and inspiration for the belief of a better tomorrow. Not only their words—but also their actions—speak volumes to our lives.

Similarly, our words have power to change circumstances and affect outcomes. Proverbs 18:21 confirms that "The tongue has the power of life and death, and those who love it will eat its fruit." That means that the words you hear and embrace can actually determine whether you live or die. If you are surrounded by positive and encouraging words, you have the potential to flourish and live. If you're surrounded by negative and discouraging words, your dreams and goals will flounder and die. That's why it is crucial to believe and to say *I can* and to avoid believing and saying *I can't*.

> THE MOMENT YOU STOP CHANGING, GROWING, AND EVOLVING, YOU ESSENTIALLY IDENTIFY THE PLACE WHERE YOU WANT TO DIE.

Not only is it important to say the right things and to do the right things, but we must also hear the right things. Unfortunately, we spend time filling our minds with the old instead of making room for the new. Our futures will be shaped by the words that are spoken over us, so make sure the words you hear and the words you speak about your life and your circumstances are positive. Don't allow your mind to become a factory that manufactures negative words and opinions, lest you be robbed of your future!

There's a popular bumper sticker that reads: "Kill Your

Television!" Considering the current state of our world, I am inclined to agree with that statement. By far, television is the most outlandish and prolific source of negative, demeaning, destructive, and derisive social commentary there is. Watching too much television has been blamed for increased violence in young people, immoral and illicit behavioral patterns, depression, and excessive criminal activity. If we are to improve the moral fabric of our society and our individual stations in life, the first course of action is to "Kill Your Television."

Remember that you can break any limitation that has been set in your life—societal, cultural, emotional, educational, environmental, or economic. It's important to remove the mental roadblocks that say you can't do something in life. You can make it. You can advance. You can progress in life. You can break human limitations of all kind. If something is part of your divine destiny and it's within your purpose for life, you can do it!

I want to end this chapter with the story of a real-life fairy tale. For years, men and women alike have been endeared by the life, contributions, and memories of Princess Diana.

Affectionately called "Princess Di," the English princess—former wife of Charles, Prince of Wales—was born on July 1, 1961, in Norfolk, England. Diana attended the exclusive West Heath boarding school in Kent for four years, but she dropped out when she was sixteen. After a term at a Swiss finishing school, she ended her formal education and got a job in London, working as a nursery-school teacher's aide. Her kind and caring disposition strongly connected with people young and old—especially those who were hurting or in need of kindness and compassion.

In February 1981, Prince Charles proposed to Diana, and the couple appeared together in public for the first time at the official engagement announcement. They were married on July 29, 1981, at St. Paul's Cathedral, in front of a congregation of 3,500. It is estimated that 750 million people worldwide watched the televised ceremony.[4]

Certainly, one of the most obvious characteristics of Princess Diana was her selfless dedication to her family and the rearing of her two sons, William (heir to the throne) and Harry. As a devoted mother, generous philanthropist, and dedicated activist in humanitarian causes, she became revered among her fellow statesmen and average citizens around the world. She became a heroine to the despondent and outcast and traveled the globe to champion the causes of those less fortunate.

Her steadfast commitment and dedication to charitable causes earned her a reputation as the "people's princess." Her calm, cool, and adoring demeanor only added to her already astonishing level of fame and adulation. But Diana's life was not without hardship. Although she lived the life of a princess, she suffered undue scrutiny from her royal family and the relentless eye of the camera, being hounded by throngs of media and paparazzi throughout her life. The deterioration of her marriage (made into a public debacle that certainly caused her grief and disdain) was prominently put on display for the world through intense media coverage.

After her separation and divorce, Diana focused her attention on such noteworthy causes as research for AIDS, breast cancer, and the banning of land mines. In June 1997, Diana auctioned off seventy-nine of her evening gowns at Christie's in New York, an event that earned more than $5.7 million for AIDS and cancer funds. To further increase awareness about the dangers of land mines, Diana traveled to such conflict-ridden areas as Angola and the former Yugoslavia on behalf of the International Campaign to Ban Landmines (the recipient of the 1997 Nobel Peace Prize).

Princess Diana died August 31, 1997, the victim of a fatal car accident. She was only thirty-six years old. The entire world mourned the passing of such a humble, kind, and caring young woman who, despite prestige and privilege, defined her plan, purpose, and destiny by meeting the needs of others.[5]

2

FEAR EQUALS FAILURE

THE WORLD IS NOT void of opportunities, nor is there any lack of talent. It is merely the presence of fear and the fear of failure that extinguish the fires of success.

In my opinion, fear is one of the most crippling forces in nature. It is a thief that robs us of our courage, our faith, our confidence, and our desire to achieve. Fear is the great silencer of success. Having faced many challenges over the years, I've learned that the best way to overcome fear is to face it.

I've heard many speakers use the word *fear* as an acronym for: False Evidence Appearing Real. Fear is the absence of faith and a tactic used to stifle our progress and success. Have you ever done something on a dare that you were otherwise afraid to do? Remember dares from grade school and high school? The more courageous you got, the more daunting the dares became. Then there were double dares and triple dares. What was it about taking on a dare from your friends that allowed you to fearlessly face your fears and accomplish the task at hand? We all know people who like challenges and delight in taking dares, but it's interesting how quickly we respond to those challenges from our friends or close acquaintances.

> YOU CAN OVERCOME YOUR FEARS BY ACTING ON YOUR FAITH.

It seems that the older we get and the more experiences we have, the more real our fears become. That's because fear is based on facts, not on faith. We are fearful because we've failed before or we've seen others fail. We are fearful because the facts tell us it's not likely that we can succeed. We are fearful because the statistics are not in our favor. We are fearful because no one has ever done it before. We are fearful because something is new and different. The truth is that you can overcome your fears by acting on your faith. Who says you can't?

Life is not a series of guaranteed successes. But even failure can be beneficial if we learn how to *fail forward*. What does it mean to fail forward? It means to use temporary setbacks and apparent failures as an opportunity to learn and grow—and to avoid making the same mistakes over and over again.

Here are four lessons I've learned about failure:

1. Don't give failure an opportunity to grow when you can water the seeds of success.

2. Failure is never final if we learn the lessons from past mistakes and correct them.

3. Failure is simply a stepping-stone to success if we learn how to *fail forward*.

4. Life's failures become the best teachers because in those moments we gain invaluable experience.

Fear equals failure. Fear is the absence of faith, and without faith it is impossible to succeed. You must have faith in yourself, in your abilities, and in your life's purpose. Fear robs people of their potential and cripples their ability to achieve greatness. So how do we overcome fear? By daring to do. Dare to do what you've been appointed to do. Dare to be successful. Dare to dream big and accomplish your goals. Dare to act on your faith. Dare to make a positive difference. By daring to do, you dramatically diminish your level of fear.

Fear's best friends are failure, doubt, and unbelief, for it is this unholy alliance that stifles growth and destroys dreams. The fear of failure holds your life hostage to mediocrity. There are many types of fear, but the result is the same: a future robbed of its potential, and an individual haunted by the mystery of *what might have been.*

There are also categories of fear: irrational and unnatural fears are known as phobias. There is fear of failure, fear of success, and fear of the unknown, to name a few. As an example for any challenges we might face, the Bible is an excellent resource and offers numerous examples of characters who exhibited courage and fearlessness in the face of great odds.

Whenever I face challenges or significant obstacles in life, I'm reminded of the story of David and Goliath, found in 1 Samuel 17.

> Now the Philistines gathered their forces for war and assembled at Socoh in Judah. They pitched camp at Ephes Dammim, between Socoh and Azekah. Saul and the Israelites assembled and camped in the Valley of Elah and drew up their battle line to meet the Philistines. The Philistines occupied one hill and the Israelites another, with the valley between them.
>
> A champion named Goliath, who was from Gath, came out of the Philistine camp. He was over nine feet tall. He had a bronze helmet on his head and wore a coat of scale armor of bronze weighing five thousand shekels; on his legs he wore bronze greaves, and a bronze javelin was slung on his back. His spear shaft was like a weaver's rod, and its iron point weighed six hundred shekels. His shield bearer went ahead of him.
>
> —1 SAMUEL 17:1–7

The story continues:

> Now David was the son of an Ephrathite named Jesse, who was from Bethlehem in Judah. Jesse had eight sons, and in Saul's time he was old and well advanced in years. Jesse's three oldest sons had followed Saul to the war: The firstborn was Eliab; the second, Abinadab; and the third, Shammah. David was the youngest. The three oldest followed Saul, but David went back and forth from Saul to tend his father's sheep at Bethlehem. For forty days the Philistine came forward every morning and evening and took his stand.... When the Israelites saw the man, they all ran from him in great fear.
> —1 SAMUEL 17:12–16, 24

WHEN OUR FOCUS IS ON LIVING MEANINGFUL AND PURPOSEFUL LIVES, FAILURE BECOMES IRRELEVANT.

Goliath was a seasoned warrior giant. David was a young shepherd. David was not a great warrior. He was a part-time shepherd boy who spent his days defending and protecting the sheep in his flock. Up until this point, he had killed a lion and a bear that were trying to steal and devour his sheep. There are some battles in life that seem to be greater than we are. Until we confront them head-on, we feel ill-prepared to wage war against the giants in our own lives. But it's important to note that each small battle prepares and propels us toward a greater encounter where God can demonstrate His power and His glory through our lives.

> Now the Israelites had been saying, "Do you see how this man keeps coming out? He comes out to defy Israel. The king will give great wealth to the man who kills him. He will also give him his daughter in marriage and will exempt his father's family from taxes in Israel."
>
> —1 SAMUEL 17:25

Often there is a huge reward for facing your fears. On the other side of confrontation with this arrogant, aggressive giant was the promise of great reward. But it required faith in God and the absence of fear for David to step up to the plate and prepare to go to war.

> Then he took his staff in his hand, chose five smooth stones from the stream, put them in the pouch of his shepherd's bag and, with his sling in his hand, approached the Philistine. Meanwhile, the Philistine, with his shield bearer in front of him, kept coming closer to David. He looked David over and saw that he was only a boy, ruddy and handsome, and he despised him. He said to David, "Am I a dog, that you come at me with sticks?" And the Philistine cursed David by his gods. "Come here," he said, "and I'll give

your flesh to the birds of the air and the beasts of the field!"

David said to the Philistine, "You come against me with sword and spear and javelin, but I come against you in the name of the LORD Almighty, the God of the armies of Israel, whom you have defied. This day the LORD will hand you over to me, and I'll strike you down and cut off your head. Today I will give the carcasses of the Philistine army to the birds of the air and the beasts of the earth, and the whole world will know that there is a God in Israel. All those gathered here will know that it is not by sword or spear that the LORD saves; for the battle is the LORD's, and he will give all of you into our hands."

WHAT FALSE EVIDENCE IS APPEARING REAL IN YOUR LIFE?

—1 SAMUEL 17:40–47

Often the fears in our lives seem enormous, and the opposition appears to be insurmountable. However, David clearly demonstrates that we need only face the fear and prepare for war. The battle belongs to God. And it is through His strength and His power that we will be victorious. Put your trust in the One who is greater than you. Allow the power of God to infiltrate your life and escort you to a higher level of existence. Open up your mind to the possibility and reality of God.

As the Philistine moved closer to attack him, David ran quickly toward the battle line to meet him. Reaching into his bag and taking out a stone, he slung it and struck the Philistine on the forehead. The stone sank into his forehead, and he fell facedown on the ground. So David triumphed over the Philistine with a sling and a stone; without a sword in his hand he struck down the Philistine and killed him. David ran and stood over him. He took hold of the Philistine's sword and drew it from the scabbard. After he killed him, he cut off his head with the sword.

—1 SAMUEL 17:48–51

Had David not faced the giant in his life, the entire Israelite army would have continued to live in fear. And while the task appeared to be daunting compared to David's abilities, it was nothing compared to God.

One of my favorite passages of Scripture is Psalm 23:4: "Even though I walk through the valley of the shadow of death, I will fear no evil, for you are with me; your rod and your staff, they comfort me." Can you imagine what it feels like to "fear no evil"? That is exactly the provision we have been given that will protect us and set us free from the bondage of fear.

Some fears are real and give us a reason to become more attentive and alert, while other fears are created in our minds through anxiety, embellishment, and exaggeration. Whether real or imagined, we are not to respond out of fear. We should recognize fear for what it is—false evidence appearing real—and use it as a catalyst to strengthen our faith.

If we allow fear to prevent us from fulfilling our purpose, then we have failed in our responsibility. But if we can demonstrate responsibility and deal with our fears, we will discover strengths and talents we didn't know we had.

Franklin D. Roosevelt said, "There is nothing to fear, but fear itself."[1] How would you live your life without the presence of fear? How would you act if you knew you could not fail? What would you do differently if you had nothing to fear? What goals would you aspire to achieve if you knew failure was not a possibility?

Examine your life, and determine if any of these following *false evidence fears* are holding you back:

- *Fear of the known*—When we rely more on facts than we do on faith, fear is bound to arise in our lives. Statistics, probabilities, predictions, and projections all serve to diminish our faith and increase our fear.

- *Fear of the unknown*—Many people live a life filled with uncertainty and the mystery of *what might have been*. We must trust that the Creator— who knows the past, present, and future—always has our best interests at heart and will not lead us into a situation that He does not prepare and equip us to face.

- *Fear of the past*—Don't allow the ghosts of the past to haunt the promise of the future. Fear of the past is a crippling ailment that prevents you from being able to move confidently toward the future. If we don't learn from our mistakes, we are bound to repeat them.

- *Fear of the future*—No one knows what tomorrow holds, except the One who created tomorrow. Research shows that more than 90 percent of the things we worry about never happen. Let's resolve to spend our time focusing on today rather than worrying about tomorrow.

- *Fear of failure*—Life is filled with failures. The first time you tried to walk, you fell down. The first time you went up to bat, you probably struck out. The key is to remember that failure is never final! Countless individuals are so afraid of the temporary embarrassment, shame, and humiliation of defeat or failure that they never even venture to try. We only fear failure if we are trying to please people. But when our focus is on living meaningful and purposeful lives, failure becomes irrelevant.

- *Fear of success*—Many people are equally as afraid of success as they are afraid of failure. For with success comes a new level of responsibility and

accountability. If you spend your life wading in
the shallow end of the pool and never venturing
into the deep, you may one day regret missing out
on the opportunity to swim.

Consider this: What if Mother Teresa had refused to dedicate
her life to service and altruism because she feared living in
poverty? What if Nelson Mandela had refused to oppose apartheid in South Africa because he feared imprisonment? What if
Dr. Martin Luther King Jr. had refused to promote civil rights
and preach a message of peace because he feared assassination?
What if Jesus had refused to accept the sins of the world and
redeem mankind because He feared dying on the cross? Where
would we be if some of the world's most
notable heroes had succumbed to fear?

One of the most well-chronicled stories
of failure and ultimate success is the life
of Abraham Lincoln. In spite of a series
of dramatic and well-publicized failures,
he went on to achieve great success and
become one of the most notable figures in
American history. Here is a brief outline
of his journey to the White House:

> IF WE ALLOW FEAR
> TO PREVENT US
> FROM FULFILLING OUR
> PURPOSE, THEN WE
> HAVE FAILED IN OUR
> RESPONSIBILITY.

- In 1816, Lincoln's family was
  forced out of their home, and he
  worked to help support them.

- In 1818, his mother died.

- In 1831, he failed in business.

- In 1832, he ran for state legislature and lost.

- In 1832, he also lost his job and was denied admittance to law school.

- In 1833, he borrowed money to start a business; it failed, and he spent seventeen years repaying the debt.

- In 1834, he ran for state legislature again—and won.

- In 1835, he was engaged to be married, but his fiancée died.

- In 1836, he suffered a total nervous breakdown and was confined to bed for six months.

- In 1843, he ran for Congress and lost.

- In 1846, he ran for Congress again and won—only to be defeated again in 1848.

- In 1856, he ran for the vice-presidential nomination and lost—receiving fewer than one hundred votes.

- In 1860, he was elected as the sixteenth president of the United States.[2]

How to Learn From Failure

- Analyze and understand how you contributed to the situation.

- Write down how you could have handled the situation differently.

- *Fail forward* and learn from your mistakes.

- Give yourself credit for having the initiative to try.

- Refuse to accept defeat.

- Ask someone who's already where you'd like to be how he or she got there.

- Pick yourself up, and try again; adjust and adapt as necessary.

- Reflect on the positive things in your life, and thank God for them.

- Surround yourself with positive influences to avoid wallowing in defeat.

- Trust that God has a purpose, plan, and process for your life.

- Remember that failure is never final.

Some people delight in failure because it's more familiar than success. Failure becomes a safety net or comfort zone, robbing people of their motivation and inspiration to achieve more. Failure loves people who fear success. But when you're called to a purpose and fail to walk in it, you'll die unfulfilled. Everyone was created with a purpose—and for a purpose. It is not only our right but also our responsibility to walk into that purpose and successfully complete it.

How many children have been told by their parents that they will never amount to anything? How many people's dreams have been ridiculed and belittled? How many people has society deemed to be failures? How many times have you failed to go forward because someone said, "You can't"? Who says you can't overcome your fears? Who says you can't defeat failure? If God didn't say it, then it's just someone else's opinion!

HERE ARE TWENTY-SIX WAYS TO FACE YOUR FEARS OR FAILURES

A—Admit that your fear is real, but pursue your dream anyway. In several recovery programs, admission of a problem is the first step to recovery. Admit that you might feel a little unnerved by the task, but commit to moving forward anyway. The best way to fight fear is to face it.

B—Boldly refuse to accept anything less than what you wan out of life. You are a divine and unique creation on the planet—deserving of the best life has to offer. Why would you settle for something you don't want—an average life filled with mediocrity? Boldly proclaim your intent to establish a better future for you and your family. Take the initiative to control your own destiny.

C—Concentrate on what you want to accomplish. Are you familiar with the phrase "a jack of all trades but a master of none"? This refers to people who do not focus on what it is they would like to accomplish. It is possible to have it all, but not all at the same time. Pick a project, a goal, or a desire, and concentrate on doing your best to obtain it.

> "THE SENSE OF OBLIGATION TO CONTINUE IS PRESENT IN ALL OF US. A DUTY TO STRIVE IS THE DUTY OF US ALL. I FELT A CALL TO THAT DUTY."[3]
> —ABRAHAM LINCOLN

D—Decide that you won't settle for less. Often we step back from our original goals if it appears that we won't meet them. Determine in your mind and settle in your heart that your dreams are worth fighting for. Decree and declare that you shall have what you say, and then go for it!

E—Elevate your thinking. Albert Einstein defined *insanity* as doing the same thing and expecting different results.[4] If you want different results, you must think and act differently to obtain them. Read a book, study a new topic, meet new people, and make new friends. Open your mind to the possibility of enlightenment outside your own world to elevate your thinking.

F—Free your mind from the garbage of the past and the unnecessary baggage of your life. Successful people travel light and avoid the excess weight of worthless emotional, mental, and spiritual junk. Focus on the positives in your life and give those negative, nay-saying doubts their walking papers.

G—Get busy. Even if you're on the right road, you'll still get run over if you just stand there doing nothing, so get busy. It takes energy and effort to make things happen. But once you take the first step, the second step becomes obvious. Momentum is created when you get into action and get busy.

H—Hope for the best. Positive thinking is crucial when undertaking any type of project. The best plan is to prepare for the worst but hope for the best. When your thoughts and actions are focused on positive outcomes in your life, your thinking attracts similar experiences. When you expect the worst, that's usually what you get.

I—Imagine your greatest potential, and then work to achieve it. If you can see it, you can be it. If you can believe it, you can achieve it. There is nothing your mind can imagine for which you don't already have the innate qualities and abilities to pursue and accomplish.

J—Jump on once-in-a-lifetime opportunities. When your ship finally comes in, make sure you're at the helm. Success is 90 percent preparation and 10 percent opportunity. When the opportunity of a lifetime comes knocking at your door, be prepared to let it in and milk it for all it's worth.

K—Keep focusing on your goals, even when it seems darkest. Remember, it's always darkest before the dawn. Countless individuals bail out and give up hope of accomplishing their goals right at the brink of success. You don't know how close you may be to the answer, finances, resources, or help you need. Keep focusing on making new strides, and you will attract the answers you need.

L—Let go of past mistakes, and focus on the future. Everyone has made mistakes, failed, and fallen short at something. So what? Someone once defined success as 99 percent failure and 1 percent perseverance. Learn from the past, let it go, and move on confidently toward your goals.

> SUCCESSFUL PEOPLE TRAVEL LIGHT AND AVOID THE EXCESS WEIGHT OF WORTHLESS EMOTIONAL, MENTAL, AND SPIRITUAL JUNK.

M—Manage your time. Don't spend major time with minor problems. We all only have twenty-four hours in a day, so it's up to each one of us to properly manage that time. Decide what's important to you and who and what is deserving of your time, for it is one of the most precious resources you have. It cannot be regained or replaced. Manage your time wisely.

N—Narrow your focus. Once you specify exactly what to accomplish, you can narrow down the choices and decisions you need to make that will help propel you toward a successful outcome. Instead of simply saying that you want to make more money next year, say that you'd like to make 20 percent more money, and save twice as much by increasing your sales and investing in a money-market account. Narrowing the playing field allows you to focus in on your target.

O—Open your mind to a new way of doing things. Just because it's always been done one way doesn't mean that's the way you have to do it. Life rewards innovation and ingenuity. Learn something new. Consider a new and different way of doing things to become more efficient and effective. Open your mind to new possibilities.

P—Plan ahead. How many times have you heard, "If you fail to plan, you plan to fail"? It's true! Planning requires the ability to envision each step of what you're trying to accomplish and to orchestrate what is required to make it happen. Don't just keep your plan in your head; write it down so others can share the vision and assist along the way.

Q—Quit second-guessing your decisions. Prior to making a decision, consider past projects that you've accomplished and their outcomes, and seek the input of other qualified and experienced individuals. Once you've considered all your options and made an objective assessment of the situation, make your decision and stick with it. A double-minded person is unstable in all his ways (James 1:8).

R—Relax. Life is too short to be taken too seriously. In the end, nobody comes out of it alive, so you might as well relax and enjoy the journey. Stress is the number-one cause of workplace illness and fatalities. Don't become another statistic of anxiety and stress. Relax and enjoy the fruits of your labor.

S—Speak positive affirmations about yourself, your family, and your life. The power of life and death is in the tongue, so it behooves you to speak positive words of support and encouragement. Those are the words that will begin to manifest themselves in your life.

T—Try something different. If you keep doing the same things, you'll keep getting the same results—at work, at home, in your marriage, and with your kids. Speak to someone you normally don't interact with, smile more, complain less, change your hairstyle or your hair color, stay up late, go to bed early, play a board game, learn a new language, start a new hobby—just try something different to experience new things.

NOTHING BEATS A FAILURE LIKE A TRY.

U—Unleash your potential. There is greatness in you, and you owe it to yourself and to others to let it shine. You'll never know how much you can accomplish until you unlock the limits on your life and unleash your potential. Don't be afraid to try something new or pursue your dreams. You only live once, so you'd better make the best of it. Give life all you have, and die empty!

V—Visualize your success. If you can see it, you can do it! Anything your mind's eye can envision, your ability can accomplish. When you begin a new project, first see yourself doing it well. Envision stepping onto the podium to address a crowd of people; visualize hitting that home run or making the game-winning shot. First see it, and then do it.

W—Worry less. It has been said that 90 percent of the things we worry about never happen. Don't allow worry and anxiety to steal that much of your time and energy. Agree to worry less and live more.

X—X-ray your motives for wanting to be successful. Are you driven by greed or revenge? If so, you're treading on dangerous territory. Make sure your motives for wanting to be successful are pure. The world is already full of treacherous, greedy, antagonistic people; we don't need any more.

Y—Yield not to temptation. There will be times in life when unethical and immoral opportunities present themselves to you. Don't wallow in the mire of compromise simply to accomplish more. Ask yourself what price you're willing to pay for your soul. What kind of example are you setting for your children or for the anonymous spectators of your life who are watching from the sidelines?

Z—Zealously go after your dreams with fervor and passion. Determine to leave a legacy of your greatness as an example for others to follow. Ask for help when you need it, and don't stop until you receive it!

DON'T MISS OUT!

Don't allow the fear of failure or of the unknown to prevent you from pursuing your goals. There's an adage that states, "Nothing beats a failure like a try." Consider the path of the fortieth U.S. president, Ronald Reagan. Who would have imagined that an actor and radio and television personality from a small town in Illinois would go on to achieve the highest leadership role in the free world—president of the United States?

> IT IS NOT ONLY OUR RIGHT BUT ALSO OUR RESPONSIBILITY TO WALK INTO OUR PURPOSE AND TO SUCCESSFULLY COMPLETE IT.

At age sixty-nine, Ronald Reagan accomplished his most significant achievement by being elected president. Prior to that he was a radio sports announcer, a film actor, and the governor of California. Reagan grew up in Dixon, Illinois, and played football in high school and at Eureka College. After graduation, he worked as a radio announcer in Iowa, eventually became one of the top sports broadcasters in the Middle West, and transitioned into the acting arena. After his discharge from the military at the end of World War II, he returned to Hollywood.

In 1964, Reagan increased his interest and participation in politics and switched to the Republican Party. In 1966, he successfully ran for the California governorship and was reelected in 1970. Reagan then sought the Republican nomination for president in 1968 and 1976 but was not nominated.

Reagan ran as the Republican Party candidate in 1980 and beat President Jimmy Carter to become the fortieth president of the United States. He was reelected to a second term in 1984.

In 1995, Reagan informed the nation and the world that he was suffering from Alzheimer's disease, an incurable condition that affects the memory. On June 5, 2004, at the age of ninety-three, Reagan died at his home, surrounded by his family. He was accorded a state funeral with full honors.[5]

Although many may differ with his political views or perspectives, there is a line of commonality among those with an opinion about President Reagan, and that is he lived his life to the fullest—demonstrating a great love of life and family and a heartfelt conviction that anything is possible, even for an actor from Illinois. Ronald Reagan was a perfect example of living a life that defied the threat of fear or failure.

3

BREAKING THE CHAINS OF STIGMA

WE LEARN ABOUT STIGMAS in our early childhood. Think back to some of the childhood stories you were told. The little engine that could was too small. The ugly duckling wasn't cute and cuddly like the other ducklings. Cinderella was a stepchild who wore rags. The seven dwarfs each had some characteristic that made them stand out from the others—not to mention the fact that they were dwarfs (often a stigma in today's society). And poor Charlie Brown could never get a break. Our world is so inundated with shallow stereotypes of who and what is acceptable that they've even overtaken our fairy tales.

In elementary schools, children are teased if they aren't wearing the right brand name of clothing. They're teased if they're too tall, too short, too skinny, too fat, or if they have straight hair, curly hair, or red hair. It seems like no one is OK anymore. We all have to be the same—to fit some unrealistic profile or standard that doesn't really exist.

But today we're going to break the chains of stigma! The word *stigma* has many definitions:

1. A distinguishing mark

2. Something that detracts from the character or reputation of a person or group

3. A disgraceful mark or characterization

In some form or another, we all have experienced the mark of a stigma from our past. Unfortunately, many people are still bound and controlled by stigmas and unable to escape the past.

STIGMA AND YOU

Perhaps words spoken to you in your youth have left you with a negative view of yourself and your life situation. You may harbor hatred, anger, spite, unforgiveness, and other damaging emotions in your heart. These things can prevent you from functioning as a healthy adult and will negatively impact your relationships with others. Why would anyone embrace these damaging emotions? Why do we allow the opinions and perceptions of others to control our lives?

You may have encountered overwhelming circumstances that placed you in debt, causing you to live in shame or financial ruin. Perhaps sickness and disease have left you mentally and physically bound, and you feel that limitations have been put on your life. Challenges you have encountered may have caused you to embrace stubbornness, greed, revenge, pride, deceit, rage, or hostility. But it is never too late to start anew, and it is never too late to change. It's never too late to break the chains of stigma off your life and begin the journey toward your predestined plan and purpose in life.

The situations may be different for each individual, but the results are the same. As a result of stigma, you are not living the full, abundant life that rightfully belongs to you. Instead, you are living in a state of denial or with the stigma of defeat as it relates to your promise and your potential.

Often it is others who hold us in bondage to the mistakes of our past and keep us from moving forward. Through guilt, doubt, and unforgiveness, many people are held hostage to the belief that they cannot re-create themselves. But once you make a commitment to break free from the chains of stigma, the old life is gone, and you are set free from your past.

Even Jesus was the product of a stigmatized life. To the natural eye, He was born out of wedlock and raised in a city equated with failure, such that the people said, "Can any good thing come out of Nazareth?" (See John 1:46.) People tried to determine Jesus's future by looking at His past and His upbringing. Jesus didn't look the way other people wanted Him to look to fulfill His purpose and destiny as Savior of the world, the Messiah. nstead of appearing as a majestic king—as the people thought He should—He entered the world as an innocent baby and lived a common life. Instead of riding on golden chariots, He rode on a lowly donkey. Instead of a grand palace, He had nowhere to lay His head or to call His own. Judging by appearances, the stigmas in the life of Jesus would render Him a failure, doomed to an unfulfilling and meaningless life. But that wasn't the case. His life has impacted countless individuals from every nation and from all walks, stations, and backgrounds in life. We must have that same commitment and conviction that regardless of our past or our upbringing, something good is going to come out of our lives!

Life demands that we live by our potential, not by our past weaknesses or failures. If we allow past stigmas to control us, we will miss the purpose for which we were born. I see the lack of motivation and fear in people who have resigned themselves to their fate. Most people feel that what has always been is what will always be. While conducting conferences and seminars around the world, I try to direct people to their potential and their strengths, but there are those who always point back to their weaknesses. When I try to show them the way forward, they are constantly looking back toward their past. In general, people don't talk about where they are, but where they were.

Holding on to the past only allows the fear of failure to cripple you and to distort the truth about your future through doubt and unbelief. Old habits, old lies, old friends, old relationships, and past experiences can keep you in the bondage. The ghosts of your past are determined to distract you from the truth and, at the same time, persuade you to rely only on what you can see around you and understand. Don't immerse your conscious mind in negativity, fear, and discouragement lest you walk into a future filled with despair and defeat.

Somebody told you something negative, and you believed it. "Oh, you will never amount to anything. You've failed once; you'll fail again. You'll never have a successful life, business, relationship, or family. Just walk away and give up because it's not going to work."

> LIFE DEMANDS THAT WE LIVE BY OUR POTENTIAL, NOT BY OUR PAST WEAKNESSES OR FAILURES.

No, that's a lie! As a result of what someone has said to you, you have created your own limitations. I believe that you can be free and that there's a way for you to come out of wherever you are.

ESCAPE THE PAST

The story of Moses is an excellent example of escaping the past and walking in purpose—as depicted in the Bible and the animated feature film *The Prince of Egypt*. When Moses was born, there was a great upheaval in the land of Egypt, and he was given away at birth in order to preserve his life. Then Moses was adopted into the home of the Egyptian pharaoh—the very one threatening to destroy him. He grew up and became a murderer, a runaway, and then a transient, wandering in the desert.

Even as a runaway, a murderer, and a displaced shepherd in the wilderness, God still called Moses and was able to use him to do a mighty work, delivering His people from bondage. Although Moses was stigmatized by a disturbing past, God called him into a new life, appointed him as a deliverer, and used him to accomplish a great task.

THE WORLD IS FULL OF BROKEN AND WOUNDED PEOPLE IN NEED OF HEALING FROM THE PAST.

It is very possible for someone with a questionable history to accomplish great things and be a blessing to their generation. Around the world, leaders and influential individuals who grew up in *dysfunctional* families, single-parent homes, or nontraditional families have managed to escape the stigma of their pasts and become successful members of society. Even individuals whose futures seem bleak and without promise can be transformed and have lives filled with meaning and purpose. If we are willing to surrender to our ultimate purpose in this life, then our knowledge, experiences, gifts, and talents can be used to accomplish what otherwise could not be done.

The reason why Moses was able to let go of the past, be rescued from his mistakes, and be used mightily during his life is because he was totally submitted to his purpose. Then and only then could Moses become the man he was destined to be. Moses wasn't limited in his life because he was an adopted child, a runaway, or an accused murderer. Instead, he saw an opportunity to be a *deliverer*. His experience and courage helped him to empathize and sympathize with those who were hurting and in pain—those just like him. He was able to look beyond what the world categorized as stigmas and focus on his potential; he lived his life with possibilities. By doing that, he was able to shake the foundations of the world and make history in the process.

From time to time, life seems to have a way of breaking you emotionally, mentally, physically, and even spiritually. If you don't take time to shake off the devastation of the past, you will never rise to victory. Some of the mental and emotional wounds that were inflicted may take years to heal. Some wounds may never completely heal. It is a sad but true statement that the world is full of broken and wounded people in need of healing from the past.

What can we do when it appears that life is kicking us down to the ground? What can we do when we feel like all hope is lost? What can we do when it seems like we've run out of options? What can we do when failure seems inevitable?

Maybe your marriage didn't work out, so you feel like you'll never be able to recover from the devastating emotional and financial loss. Maybe you lost your job and you think you'll never find another one. Maybe you made the wrong choice and your decisions are coming back to haunt you. Maybe the mistakes you made in the past seem to keep you from moving ahead into the future. Please understand that no one in life is exempt from adversity. Don't be fooled by wealthy athletes and celebrities who appear to have the best of everything. Make no mistake...money does not exempt one from adversity and unhappiness. In many cases, it creates more. But regardless of the situation, there is hope. We have the assurance of knowing that our current situation does not have to be our future predicament; that what we see now is not what will always be.

> NO ONE IN LIFE IS EXEMPT FROM ADVERSITY.

Whether your current problems were brought on through no fault of your own, or whether they are a direct consequence of your actions and decisions, the way out is the same. First, we must acknowledge that what is in the past *is past*. No person on earth can change or undo the past, so our best option is to focus on the present and make better decisions that will affect our future.

Here are four things to remember about the past:

1. The past is over, and there is nothing you can do to change it now.

2. Dwelling on past mistakes doesn't fix them; it merely hinders your ability to focus on the present and to plan for the future.

3. Learning from the past helps you to avoid making the same mistakes; those who don't learn from the past are destined to repeat it.

4. Yesterday is history, tomorrow is a mystery, but today is a gift; that's why we call it the present.

Can't you just imagine that when Moses returned to Egypt forty years later, there was still someone whispering behind his back: "Hey, isn't that Moses—the child who was adopted and raised in the palace? You know, I heard he killed a man a few years ago. I wonder what he's doing here. If I were him, I'd be ashamed to show my face." Even after we've paid our debt to society, even after we've repented and received forgiveness from God, someone is going to try to remind us of the past. Who says you have to be held hostage to your past? If God didn't say it, then it's just someone else's opinion.

Les Brown is one of the most well-known and successful motivational speakers in the world. To hear his testimony and appreciate the obstacles he had to overcome is encouraging and reassuring to all who hear his story. Les was born on the floor in an abandoned building in a low-income section of Miami, Florida. He and his twin brother were given away for adoption. In elementary school he was labeled "Educable Mentally Retarded (EMR)" and held back a grade. As a youngster, he was picked on in school and called the "dumb twin" because of his academic failings. Because of his meager upbringing and less-than-desirable surroundings, he encountered many naysayers who thought his dreams of becoming a motivational speaker were outrageous.

But for every discouraging word that was spoken, Les was encouraged to pursue his dreams by a mentor who understood faith and the power of positive thinking. Even on his dramatic rise to fame and fortune, Les encountered numerous setbacks and disappointments along the way, including the cancellation of his television talk show, the death of his mother (adopted mother who raised him from infancy), a divorce, and a medical diagnosis of prostate cancer.[1]

Any one of those events would be enough to send a person spiraling into the depths of depression and despair. So, what has kept Les Brown on top, traveling around the world and motivating others toward greatness? Consider this excerpt from his book, *It's Not Over Until You Win*:

> Self-realization and self-awareness are vital to our lives. You feel the way you feel because of the thoughts you are thinking. If you are feeling down and out, nearly every thought that comes into your head will be colored by negativity. Often when you have been knocked down by life, you tend to see only the worst in people, situations, and in your options. You feel hopelessness. Notice that I have not said that your life is hopeless, only that you feel that way. You should not make the mistake of thinking that your feelings reflect the reality.

We cannot always control the thoughts that come into our minds, but we can control the thoughts that we dwell on. During the down times, we have to monitor our thoughts and eliminate those that drag us down while embracing those that elevate our moods.

In hard times, your life can get stalled or it can get propelled. It depends on whether you allow negative thoughts and emotions to dominate your actions, or whether you control your thoughts and actions in spite of your emotions.[2]

Those are powerful words and a powerful testimony too! Just imagine the joy of being able to break free from our limitations—the invisible line drawn in the sand of our minds, or in our spirits, that says *you can't.* Who says we can't overcome? Who says we can't be healthy? Who says we can't regain our losses and be restored? Who says we can't be debt free? Who says we can't make it to the top? Remember: if God didn't say it, then it's just someone else's opinion.

It's never too late to break the chains of stigma off your life.

My response is this: Whether you believe in God or not, there is still a divine plan, purpose, and destiny for your life. And during times of adversity, it is necessary—not to mention therapeutic—to believe in something or someone greater

A QUESTION I OFTEN ENCOUNTER FROM PEOPLE AROUND THE WORLD IS, "WHO DO I TURN TO IF I DON'T BELIEVE IN GOD?"

than yourself. If there is someone whose life inspires you and whose principles reflect the positive possibilities and potential that you desire, find out what that person believes and seek to understand what gives him or her the hope, power, and motivation to continue. Do your research and analyze what other successful, inspirational, and influential people have learned along life's journey. Take some time to listen, reflect, and pray.

Observe the signals that life is sending you, and allow yourself to submit to the purpose, plan, and destiny for your life.

OBSERVE THE SIGNALS THAT LIFE IS SENDING YOU, AND ALLOW YOURSELF TO SUBMIT TO THE PURPOSE, PLAN, AND DESTINY FOR YOUR LIFE.

Read Philippians 4:13, and study what it says: "I can do everything through him who gives me strength." The word *everything* refers to spiritual and natural things. That means you can do anything spiritual and anything natural. That means that in this life, you have the ability to overcome spiritual, emotional, mental, physical, and financial limitations. You have access to supernatural power, and you've been endowed with certain strengths that people around you can observe. These strengths have the ability, the force, and the power to overcome any challenge or obstacle that is set before you. It is inherently a part of who you are, so don't shortchange your life—tap into your potential instead.

But how do you overcome stigmas, adversity, and past failures? And what if you don't feel like you can? Understand that you cannot overcome what you run away from. When adversity is staring you in the face, don't back away from it—confront it. It takes courage, but, more importantly, it takes a belief in yourself that says *I can*.

4

GARBAGE, BAGGAGE, OR LUGGAGE

GARBAGE, BAGGAGE, OR LUGGAGE—what are you carrying around with you?

Garbage—n. 1) waste, as from a market or kitchen; 2) something that is thrown away; 3) anything that is worthless or unnecessary.

Baggage—n. 1) the trunks, bags, and other equipment of a traveler; 2) burdensome, superfluous, or outdated ideas and practices.

Luggage—n. 1) suitcases, valises, or trunks; 2) containers used for transporting clothing and other personal items during travel.

God can change your heart, but it's up to you to change your mind. Are you willing to throw out the garbage and baggage in your life that's holding you back? Are you ready to let go of some unhealthy and unprofitable emotions, relationships, and habits? Are you willing to change your life? Who says you can't? God says you can!

HOW TO RECOGNIZE GARBAGE

Garbage stinks. Is there something in your life that stinks? Maybe it's a dead relationship that you're still dragging around, trying to revive. Maybe it's a mistake from your past that you should have let go of and thrown out days, weeks, months, or years ago. Could it be an addictive habit that's destroying your ability to make good decisions? Or maybe it is a bad attitude that offends those around you. Whatever the source may be, it's time to throw it out.

Garbage attracts pests and parasites. Have you ever noticed that nothing attractive congregates around garbage? Garbage doesn't attract flowers, eagles, or swans; it attracts mold, maggots, flies, roaches, rats, and vultures. In real life, these pests and parasites feed off death and waste, and the same concept is true for your life. If you are surrounded by garbage, you can expect parasites, moochers, and leeches—disguised as friends—to show up soon. Don't expect successful, motivated, and empowered people to show up in your life if it's filled with garbage.

Garbage festers. Anger, bitterness, and unforgiveness are emotions and characteristics that fester. That means that given a chance, these attributes will not only cause rot and decay in your emotional life, but they will also slowly infect those around you. These types of situations do not heal and go away on their own. You must make a conscious effort to clean them up and put them out of your life. People who speak doubt and unbelief as well as those who harbor anger and unforgiveness risk damaging themselves physically, mentally, and emotionally as a result of harboring these festering vices.

Garbage does not improve with time. The saying goes, "Some things get better with time." Garbage is not one of them. The longer you allow garbage to sit around in your life, the worse it smells, the more garbage it creates, and the harder it is to rid yourself of it. For example, if you forget to take out the trash and instead leave it sitting, when

DON'T DRAG THE PAST INTO YOUR FUTURE, BECAUSE THE PAST IS SIMPLY EXCESS BAGGAGE THAT IS FILLED WITH GARBAGE.

you return, you will have a bigger mess than when you left. This is also the case for emotional and lifestyle garbage. For instance, what started out as an unnecessary snide remark escalates into an argument. Then the argument turns into a fight, and the fight later develops into a feud. If left unchecked, a feud turns into anger and hatred, resulting in hurt feelings and damaged relationships, all of which could have been avoided if someone had simply walked away and thrown out the garbage.

THE VAST MAJORITY OF HEROES AND REVOLUTIONARIES OF OUR TIME LIVE A LIFE BASED ON LOVE AND HUMILITY.

Garbage rots. When something rots, it breaks down and begins to decompose. Are there parts of your life breaking down, falling apart, or decomposing? The longer garbage is left exposed, the unhealthier it becomes. What issues in your life need to be addressed and put away before they begin to rot? Whom do you need to forgive or receive forgiveness from? To whom do you owe an apology? Who deserves more of your time? Whom can you compliment or encourage? Don't allow the relationships in your life to rot.

HOW TO RECOGNIZE BAGGAGE

Baggage is unnecessary. Have you ever traveled with someone who carries way too much stuff? Getting from point A to point B is difficult because that person is dragging unnecessary junk that slows him or her down. Many of us are carrying around unnecessary junk from the past—guilt, shame, unforgiveness, and other unresolved issues. When you travel, there are some things you don't need to take with you. Similarly, when you're progressing in life, there are some things that should be left behind. As we stated earlier, yesterday is history, tomorrow is a mystery, but today is a gift; that's why we call it the present. Unpack the baggage of yesterday's history, and don't start packing for tomorrow's mystery. Travel lightly, and take one day at a time.

Baggage is heavy. Imagine walking up a hill, carrying a hundred-pound pack on your back. Then imagine constantly adding weight to that pack with each additional step. That's what it's like to carry around the past with you instead of leaving it behind. Instead of lightening your load by discarding unnecessary memories and thoughts from the past, we hold on to those old emotions and add on additional weight to carry. Eventually, we become burdened down and unable to move at all. Don't allow the burdens of life to immobilize you. Unpack your bags, and move forward.

Baggage is excessive and disorganized. Have you ever accidentally thrown something in the trash can and then had to go digging in afterward to look for it? The orange peels are mixed in with the dinner scraps. The eggshells somehow landed among the laundry lint. Not pleasant, right? It's the same way with life's baggage. There is no rhyme or reason with baggage. Everything is just thrown in together with no semblance of order. There's just a whole lot of trash that you have to weed through. Personal and mental baggage can be excessive. We should do a weekly or monthly *baggage check* to make sure we've discarded the necessary items and can easily locate those things of value.

Baggage is inefficient. Ever notice how difficult it is to find something in the attic of your home? At work we have important files tucked neatly away in secure file cabinets. And when we need to access guarded information, we at least have an idea of where to start. But what if you go looking for some lost relic up in the attic or in the back of your closet? It's not likely that you would find it in an effective or efficient manner. While we're looking, we usually find several other lost items that get misplaced in the excess baggage from our lives. Mental baggage contains the excess stores of junk we don't need and can't use. Commit to cleaning out your closet and discarding excessive, useless baggage in your life.

> DON'T DRAG THE PAST INTO YOUR FUTURE, BECAUSE THE PAST IS SIMPLY EXCESS BAGGAGE THAT IS FILLED WITH GARBAGE.

Now that you know how to recognize garbage and baggage, what can you do to remove it from your life? Remember the *Peanuts* character Pigpen? Everywhere he went there was a cloud of dirt and dust swirling around him. That's how some of our lives are. We travel through life with dirt and filth from the past, dust from unresolved issues, lint and debris from failed relationships. Much like Pigpen's cloud, we carry this garbage with us everywhere we go, and all of it is distorting our view of a better and brighter future. How much better it would be to get rid of garbage and baggage so that the only luggage we travel through life with is the blessings of God's destiny for our lives.

How to Get Rid of Garbage and Baggage

Take an inventory of the people you spend most of your time with.

Are the people positive, motivated, and moving toward admirable goals in life? Are the individuals with whom you spend the most time helping propel you toward your God-given purpose in life, or are they physically, financially, emotionally, and spiritually draining you? Friendships and relationships should be mutually beneficial for all parties involved. If you're associating with individuals who take more out of you than they pour back into your life—and vice versa—consider altering where and how you spend your time.

Take an inventory of where and how you spend your time.

Do you frequent bars and nightclubs and spend countless hours on the phone gossiping or chatting online? Or do you volunteer in the community, helping students with their homework after school and delivering meals to the elderly? The point is not to totally eliminate social functions and recreation, but to take an inventory of your life. Simply consider whether or not you spend time making a positive contribution to society.

Think of any event that makes you angry or frustrated.

How long ago did it happen? Have you tried to remedy the situation in a positive and mature manner that demonstrates love and forgiveness? Have you sincerely prayed about the situation and asked for a solution? These approaches are generally more effective than carrying around excess anger, frustration, hatred, and condemnation. The vast majority of heroes and revolutionaries of our time live a life based on love and humility. What a powerful example of how we should live our lives. What would happen if you apologized first—regardless of whether you were right or wrong? What if you chose to forgive someone instead of holding that person's mistakes against him or her? What if you chose to help someone without judging or condemning that person for going astray? These are classic ways of eliminating garbage and baggage from your life.

WHAT ISSUES
IN YOUR LIFE
NEED TO BE
ADDRESSED
AND PUT AWAY
BEFORE THEY
BEGIN TO ROT?

Release your anger.

There are times when we will get angry, but it is both unhealthy and counterproductive to harbor that anger and resentment. In some form or another, the results of those repressed emotions will be released. It's OK to be angry when you are wronged, but it is not OK to remain angry and hold on to those negative emotions.

A friend of mine in North Carolina has what she calls a twenty-four-hour rule. No matter how upset she is, she resolves to do something positive regarding the situation within twenty-four hours. This is what she shared with me:

Kingsley, I remember not too long ago I came very close to dying. At that moment I realized that the only thing that mattered in life was that my soul belonged to God. Not one day on this earth is promised to us, and I didn't want to waste my last ones being angry and resentful. How long do I want God to remember my sins and hold them against me? Then how can I expect forgiveness from God and not give it to others in return? Once I realized I was going to live, I made a conscious decision that not another day in my life would be wasted on useless, irrelevant, negative emotional garbage. Whatever the situation may be, I give myself twenty-four hours to express what I feel—be it anger, resentment, sadness, frustration or disappointment. Then I make a conscious choice to pray, forgive someone, apologize, or make the situation right. That doesn't mean the hurt goes away in twenty-four hours; it simply means I find something positive or productive to do regarding the situation within those twenty-four hours. Anger, bitterness, and frustration—especially unforgiveness—are emotions that do more damage to the one who holds them than to the victim they are poured upon. No matter how angry I get, eventually I'm going to have to let it go. So, if I'm going to let it go anyway, it might as well be today. There's a popular saying in modern psychology, "Do you want to be right, or do you want to be happy?" Each day I make a choice to be happy.

Her powerful testimony really blessed me. We can all make a choice to be happy and joyful by the grace of God. Whatever the situation may be, ask yourself if it will matter one year from now. If the answer is yes, what positive steps can you take to resolve the issue? If the answer is no, it won't matter one year from now. Ask yourself another question: Will it matter one month from now? And if it won't matter in a month, it probably won't matter in a week. And if it won't matter in a week, it won't matter in a day. And if it won't matter in a day, it probably doesn't matter at all.

> YESTERDAY IS HISTORY, TOMORROW IS A MYSTERY, BUT TODAY IS A GIFT; THAT'S WHY WE CALL IT THE PRESENT.

Make a list of ten bad habits you have and ten good habits you'd like to have. Each week, choose a different habit from each list to exchange. For example, every time you get ready to curse or swear, instead smile or give someone a compliment. Here's another example: Every time you exhibit road rage (angrily blaring the horn or cutting someone off in traffic), slowly count backward from ten to zero, and then say a prayer for the person instead. Ask for forgiveness for your anger, and then forgive that person for whatever mistake he or she might have made. Finally, every time you're late for a meeting or an appointment, send the person or persons with whom you were to meet a thank-you card expressing your appreciation for their time and your apology for being late. If every time you do something negative you replace it with something positive, eventually your new positive habits will replace the old negative ones.

Garbage is the remnants and leftovers of the past, the dying decaying parts of your life that are of no value. Don't drag the past into your future, because the past is simply excess baggage that is filled with garbage. Throw out the garbage, throw out the baggage, and fill your new luggage with the wonderful promises of a blessed present and even brighter future.

5

WHO SAYS YOU CAN?

ONE OF THE PEOPLE I most respect and appreciate for his *can do* attitude is former secretary of state General Colin Powell. Not only has his life demonstrated incredible achievements, integrity, and acts of courage, but he also inspires others to do the same.

Before becoming secretary of state, Colin Powell served as a key aide to the secretary of defense and as national security advisor. He also served thirty-five years in the United States Army, rising to the rank of four-star general and serving as chairman of the joint chiefs of staff. Outside of his well-decorated military service and political career, Powell is a man of great conviction, whose dedication to educating and improving the lives of young people is remarkable. A man of profound wisdom, Powell often says, "Do the right thing, even when you get no credit for it. Do the right thing when no one is watching or will ever know about it. You will always know. There are no secrets to success. It is the result of preparation, hard work, and learning from failure."[1]

Dr. Myles Munroe said it this way:

> Your life has the potential to fulfill your purpose. If, however, you imprison that potential, you rob your life of its purpose and fulfillment. You and every other individual on this planet possess an awesome treasure. Too much of this treasure is buried every day, untapped and untouched, in the cemeteries of our world. Much talent, skill and creativity have been lost to the world for want of a little courage. Many obscure men and women enter eternity pregnant with potential, with a stillborn purpose. Living with ability brings responsibility. Dying with ability reveals irresponsibility.[2]

Life is full of possibilities—both positive and negative. If you want to be negative, it's possible. If you want to be positive, it's possible. If you want to believe in a lie, it's possible, and if you want to believe in truth, it's possible. Life is full of possibilities.

But when you choose to pursue the possibility of negative things, or negativism, don't try to drag people who want to think positively along with you. It's true that misery loves company, but don't try to drag your spouse, sons, daughters, brothers, sisters, church members, co-workers, uncles, aunts, and your parents along with you. If you choose to go this route, it's up to you. Failure is contagious. You can get it by birth, by inheritance, by association, or by transference. Show me the kind of people you hang around, and I can tell you what kind of person you're going to become. In spite of what you've heard, in spite of what you've learned, and in spite of what you know, open your mind to possibility thinking.

Imagine what the world would be like if nobody ever ventured to think, "It's possible." No one would have sailed around the world for fear of falling off the edge of what was believed to be a flat planet. No one would have ever walked on the moon. No one would have ever discovered the drug penicillin. No one would have invented the light bulb, telephone, airplane, automobile, television, camera, or computer.

WHEN YOU CONSIDER THE POTENTIAL AND POSSIBILITIES OF YOUR LIFE, YOU IMMEDIATELY UNDERSTAND THAT IN SPITE OF YOUR PAST, YOU CAN.

Begin to change the way you think. You can change things; you can change a negative life to a positive life. You can change a negative, defeated attitude to a happy, healthy, optimistic outlook on life. It's all up to you. In his book

Tough Times Never Last, But Tough People Do!, Dr. Robert Schuller explains the art of *possibility thinking*. He describes it as the management of ideas and the creation of possibilities to accomplish your goals. Impossibility thinkers are those who instinctively look for reasons why something can't be done—the naysayers and doubters. The possibility thinkers are those who instinctively look for the promise of potential in any problem—those who apply ingenuity and innovation to create positive solutions.[3]

REFUSE TO ACCEPT ANYTHING LESS THAN GOD'S BEST FOR YOUR LIFE.

One of the trademark formulas in possibility thinking is, "Count to ten and win." Schuller encourages readers facing any difficult challenge or seemingly hopeless situation to create ten possibilities to solve a problem. Suddenly—as if by divine inspiration—impossibilities become possibilities right before your eyes.

Everything is possible for the person who believes. You are capable of responding to the possibilities of life. You are capable of responding to the possibility of being healthy, the possibility of being rich, of being optimistic, being strong, being peaceful, or being joyful. It's up to you, and it's in you; that is your free will. Your capability is your free will, and your capability is based on information, or the knowledge and understanding you have about something.

Some people may think that because of their past mistakes or their upbringing, they cannot fulfill their destinies or have an impact on someone else's life. But that is not the case. When you consider the potential and possibilities of your life, you immediately understand that in spite of your past, *you can.*

The moment we lose sight of who we are and the potential and purpose that's in us, defeat becomes a possibility. When we suppress the authority of God in our lives and allow outside influences to negatively impact our thoughts, failure becomes a possibility. Whenever you feel you are going through the valley, don't be confused by what you see in front of you. A hill only looks like a mountain when you're in the valley. We all have low periods in our lives from time to time, but we cannot allow those temporary moments of discouragement to disguise the reality of goodness and the possibility of blessings in our future.

I Dare You...

Dare to dream, dare to achieve, dare to try, dare to overcome, dare to be, dare to do! Right this moment, I want you to make a commitment to yourself that you're going to be the best possible *you* that you can be. No more excuses. No more delays. No more denials. No more doubts. No more fears. No more failures. No more. Just simply decide that you can do it because you believe you can.

Create a vision for your life, and then follow it. Describe what your life looks like a month from now, a year from now, a decade from now. What things do you want to change? What do you want to do differently? How to you want to leave your mark on this world? What is your legacy?

Who are your role models, mentors, or sources of inspiration? Contact them, compliment them, let them know that you appreciate their contributions to the world. Even heroes need encouragement. Kiss the kids, hug the dog, make dinner for your spouse—vow to be a better version of you than you've been in the past. Become the change you want to see in your life, in your community, in the world.

Expect to achieve nothing less than success. Mediocrity is beneath you, so don't allow the clouds of failure and compromise to fool you into settling for less than your God-given right to excel in life. If you don't try, who will? If you don't go, who will? If not you, then who?

Pronounce a benediction on the negativity of doubt, fear, and failure in your life. Make a list of every discouraging lie that has impeded your progress or hindered your momentum, and pronounce a benediction over it. Then bury it, burn it, or shred it; just destroy the dream-snatching, joy-stealing, guilt-ridden garbage from your past, and vow never to look back. Then proceed full-steam ahead.

Become your own biggest cheerleader and fan. Don't wait for someone else to encourage you—encourage yourself. Don't wait for someone to give you a pat on the back; you may have to wait too long. Don't wait for someone else to recognize your contributions; just go about the business of doing, being, giving, loving, and sharing, and the recognition for your efforts will find its way to you. In the meantime, simply do good for the sake of doing good.

Every plan, vision, and purpose for your life has already been predestined for you. Seek to know the One who created you and assigned your purpose to help you fulfill your life's calling. Tithe of your talent, time, and resources, and watch the increase come back to you. Make the world a better place for others, and see if it doesn't improve for you. Pave the way for someone else, and delight in how the road to success will rise up to meet your feet.

> PRONOUNCE A BENEDICTION ON THE NEGATIVITY OF DOUBT, FEAR, AND FAILURE IN YOUR LIFE.

Refuse to accept anything less than God's best for your life. Who says you can't be happy? Who says you can't be successful? Who says you can't be healthy? Who says you can't be prosperous? Who says you can't be free? Who says you can't fulfill your divine purpose in life?

6

PURPOSE, PLAN, AND PROCESS

ASK YOURSELF THIS QUESTION: "Have I arrived in life, or am I still on the journey?" For most of us, the answer is that we are still on the journey, because it's a never-ending progression toward a higher calling and purpose. It's important to know there is a divine purpose, plan, and process that have been orchestrated just for you.

Your purpose in life is accomplished by knowing *what* to do, *when* to do it, *where* to do it, *how* to do it, *why* you're doing it, and *for whom* you're doing it. If you don't act with a sense of confidence and direction, you will basically wander aimlessly through life never fulfilling your purpose. I once heard a speaker say that most people are just wandering generalities with no purpose or direction in life.

In his book *Releasing Your Potential,* my good friend Dr. Myles Munroe states:

> The next generation needs the treasure of your potential. Think of the many inventions, books, songs, works of art and great accomplishments others in past generations have left for you. Even as their treasures have become your blessings, so your treasures must become your children's unborn children's blessings. You must not die unfinished and let the grave steal the gems of the future. Deliver your potential to inspire the children of our world to release theirs.
>
> The essence of potential is not preservation but liberation. Although we cannot change the past, we have the potential to chart our destiny and arrange a better future for our children. The opportunity to blame others for the past is often before us; but we can never transfer responsibility for the future to others. You and I have been given by God all that we need to fulfill His purpose for our lives. We possess the ability to impact our homes, our communities, our cities, our nations and perhaps the world if we

dare to challenge ourselves and place demands on the vast wealth of potential buried deep within us.

Decide today to do something with your dreams. Disappoint procrastination and commit yourself to releasing your potential. Stop wishing and start willing. Stop proposing and start purposing. Stop procrastinating and start planning. Determine to die empty and leave the earth an inheritance that gives life to others. Remember, few things are impossible to diligence and skill. Great works are performed by perseverance.

The fact that you were born is evidence that you possess something that can benefit the world.

God gave you potential for the blessing of future generations.

The greatest need of ability is responsibility.

God places demands on your potential by giving your ability responsibility.

Fulfillment is directly related to the successful completion of a task.

God has given you everything you need to fulfill His purpose for your life.[1]

PURPOSE

Knowing your purpose in life gives you a renewed sense of confidence and direction in your words and actions. Every person on the planet was born into this world with a divine purpose that only that person can fulfill. Many will never discover their life's purpose because they have been distracted by the adversities of life and discouraged from pursuing their dreams. However, the consequence of living a life without purpose is leading a futile existence and dying unfulfilled. There is no act of creation—past or present—that does not accomplish a divine purpose. Remember that regardless of the circumstances, your life is not a mistake. When you discover your life's calling and recognize the potential within to uplift and inspire others to greatness, honoring the Creator, you will experience an emotional and spiritual fulfillment that cannot be measured or explained.

PLAN

The character Hannibal from the mid-1980s television show *The A-Team*, frequently would say, "I love it when a plan comes together." Well, when you commit to seeking and fulfilling your divine purpose in life, you will find that every experience—positive or negative—will come together in a perfectly laid plan to assist in the execution of what you alone have been called to do in this world. The divine plan for your life is actually a road map leading to your destiny. It is expected and allowed that we will falter and make mistakes along the way. However, there is a basic understanding that we will commit to following our life's plan and accomplish our goals. Upon choosing to follow the path that is destined for our lives, we have a guarantee that *the plan will come together*. No remnants from your past, attacks from your adversaries, or adversities in life can overthrow or thwart the unique plan that has been developed for you to follow.

PROCESS

The road to success is filled with ups and downs, and the process for fulfilling your purpose is an exciting and inspirational journey. Most of us would prefer to have a life defined by smooth sailing, minimal confrontation, and no adversity. Nobody wants or likes to suffer. However, that is an unrealistic expectation and tends to give a false sense of hope and reality. The very process by which we are prepared to pursue our purpose is filled with trials, triumphs, defeats, and failures. It is through this process of strengthening and refining that we understand the importance of purpose. The processes put in place to prepare us for service in this world are usually not the ones we would have chosen. As a matter of fact, we would probably try to avoid them altogether. Ultimately, we understand and appreciate the purpose, plan, and process for our lives and embrace our true calling.

Failure, success, blessings, curses, joy, sadness, happiness, contentment, loneliness, or whatever you might be feeling and experiencing have all been subliminally implanted into your subconscious by the thoughts, words, and influences that surround you. We all make a conscious choice to pursue our purpose, follow God's plan, and endure the process that has been laid before us. An old Native American tale says, "An older wise chief is talking to his grandson about the meaning of life. He tells the boy, 'There are two wolves warring inside me. One is driven by hatred, anger, greed, selfishness, fear, and defeat. The other is driven by love, peace, joy, humility, kindness, and compassion.' Intrigued, the little boy asks, 'Grandfather, which wolf will win?' To which the old chief replies, 'Whichever one I feed.'"[2]

Sometimes life catches us off guard, and it seems that the experiences we encounter cannot possibly be working for our good. But rest assured that life is not some haphazard sequence of events with no plan or purpose. You are not randomly wandering on this journey called *life* with no final destination. You have a plan, purpose, and destiny designed by a Creator who is omniscient and omnipotent (all knowing and all powerful). Therefore anything that you encounter along the journey toward fulfilling your purpose has been ordained and predestined to occur. "And we know that in all things God works for the good of those who love him, who have been called according to his purpose" (Rom. 8:28).

> IF YOU THINK YOU CAN, OR YOU THINK YOU CAN'T, EITHER WAY YOU'RE RIGHT.

When you identify and accept the vision or a plan for your life, be very careful with whom you share it. The world is full of dream snatchers who lie in wait for the right moment to dash your hopes and quench your spirits. Les Brown once said, "Some people are so negative, if you put them in a darkroom, they'll develop."[3] Unfortunately, he's right. I've learned from years of experience to stop sharing my dreams with small-minded, negative people. When I set my goals, I set them high. I think big thoughts and dream big dreams. I figure, if you're going to be thinking anyway, you might as well think big!

A popular quotation says, "If you don't know where you're going, any road will take you there." That's why it's important not only to understand your purpose but also to know where you're headed and what your final destination will be. Both in the natural and in the spiritual realm, everyone should have a purpose, plan, and process for his or her life. Your purpose defines your primary reason for living, the intrinsic nature of your being, and your driving force in life. Your plan dictates how you will accomplish your purpose. It outlines your strategies and tactics—education, career, associations, relationships, and priorities. The process helps organize and prioritize your actions, preparing you for the journey, increasing your faith, and enhancing your ability to endure.

Do you know who you were created to be? Do you understand why you were put on this earth? Do you really understand how much your life impacts those around you and how the purpose of your life is intertwined with others? Not fulfilling your appointed role in life may hinder the progress of someone else. If you refuse to be a teacher, you risk disappointing the students who could have learned from you. If you refuse to go back to school and become a doctor, you risk losing the patients whom your life was supposed to touch. What if every mom and dad decided that the role of a parent was too much to undertake? There would be generations of lost children with no hope or expectation for anything better in life. Destiny belongs to everyone, but your destiny belongs uniquely to you.

Begin to think of yourself differently—envision yourself not as a lowly individual just making do in life, but as a person with a plan, purpose, and destiny. Understand that you play a key role in the universe and that no one can replace your unique position in this divine design. When you know the truth of who you are, there is not a sense of arrogance but one of humility. Humility is acknowledging that there is an authority above you and that your call is to service—to your Creator and to others. Humility gives you the grace of learning and growing. Humility is not destructive or demeaning; it is an honor and a blessing and a distinction that few can proclaim.

> NOT FULFILLING YOUR APPOINTED ROLE IN LIFE MAY HINDER THE PROGRESS OF SOMEONE ELSE.

I would be remiss if I didn't explain the role and power of prayer in pursuing the divine purpose, plan, and process for your life. As you know, prayer is communicating with God to accomplish His divine will. Prayer isn't simply asking Him to supply a laundry list of your wants and desires. Neither is it crying and complaining about what's wrong in your life. Prayer is an intimate conversation with the Creator to share the contents of your heart and to receive divine insight and guidance regarding the ultimate plan for your life.

Know What to Do

It's important to know that even when you know your plan, purpose, and destiny, difficult times will still arise, and there will be times when you simply don't know which way to go or what to do. When—not if—that time comes, here are five things to keep in mind (taken from 2 Chronicles 20):

1. *Stand*—Stand firmly on the last correct decision you've made, and analyze the situation from that point. Even if you're afraid, don't run away or attempt to ignore the situation. You may not need to make a quick decision, but you do need to confront the issues. Find strength and comfort in a resource that has proven to be effective in the past (Bible passages, prayers, meditations, and so forth), and use it as an anchor to stand your ground.

2. *Focus*—Set your eyes on the creative power that lies within. Don't dwell on the problem; focus on the solution. Maybe you can't solve everything in one day, but you can accomplish something each day. Focus on finding solutions the same way you eat an elephant—one bite at a time.

3. *Reflect and meditate*—Take time to clear your mind of clutter, and allow the answers for your life to speak to you. Often, we are so overwhelmed and overly concerned about the

problems that we look right past the answers. Reflection and meditation require quiet time and peace. You cannot effectively reflect or meditate in between meetings, errands, or while you're doing household chores. Find a quiet place, and reflect on literature that nourishes your mind and soul. Meditate on the presence of peace, and allow your mind to rest and renew itself to resolve the matters of the day.

4. *Express gratitude*—It's hard to be thankful and negative at the same time, so use this method to change your unpleasant attitude and environment into a pleasant one. Even during a difficult situation, it's imperative to find something to be grateful for because it allows you to redirect positive energy in a meaningful way. As the cliché says, it could always be worse. But as we learned, the power of life and death is in the words we speak, so choose them carefully.

5. *Remain committed*—Don't allow doubt and discouragement to fool you into prematurely giving up on your goals. It's not necessary for you to have all the answers, but it is necessary for you to stay the course and weather the storm. You have to stay in the race in order to win it. Against all odds, face the challenges and remain committed to your goals.

Sometimes the ultimate purpose for our lives is immediately evident and on display for all to see. There are natural-born leaders, there are humanitarians and philanthropists, and there are those who are blessed with extraordinary gifts and talents. Individuals like Mahatma Gandhi, Mother Teresa, and Nelson Mandela seemed perfectly fitted for the lifelong calling of service and sacrifice on behalf of those who are oppressed. For others, the purpose of life unfolds in layers, like a rose bud, with each petal of purpose slowly being revealed.

Just because the vision for your life doesn't materialize when you expect it to, or arrive in the manner you anticipated, doesn't mean the value of the call to destiny isn't just as great. Some are called to a lifetime of commitment and purpose, while others are called to a season of service or a specific moment in time.

I feel almost certain that as a little girl, Sheila Johnson never imagined that she would be the first African American female billionaire. Along with her ex-husband, Robert Johnson, the former music teacher, she cofounded BET (Black Entertainment Television) on cable television, giving her access and influence to millions of lives through the medium of entertainment. Through years of hard work and sacrifice, they were able to build a multimedia conglomerate and profit from its success. A savvy businesswoman and dedicated mother, Johnson is an entrepreneur, single parent, philanthropist, and civic leader—positioned in the top percentage of the wealthiest people in the world.[4]

Consider the life of media mogul and female billionaire Oprah Winfrey. Although most little girls stand in front of the mirror with visions of grandeur holding a hairbrush-turned-microphone, few are able to make the transition from make-believe to monumental success. But that is the story of Oprah Winfrey, television host, producer, actress, entrepreneur, philanthropist, and one of the world's most beloved celebrities.

Winfrey was born in 1954 and raised by her grandmother on a farm with no indoor plumbing in Kosciusko, Mississippi. Her love for books and public speaking gained her a educational scholarship and paved the way for a career in broadcasting. While still in high school, she became the youngest person and the first African American woman to anchor the news at the Nashville, Tennessee, radio station WTVF-TV. In 1984 she moved to Chicago to host WLS-TV's morning talk show, *AM Chicago*, which became the number-one local talk show just one month after she began. *The Oprah Winfrey Show* entered national syndication in 1986 and became the highest-rated talk show in television history. Currently, it is estimated that her show is seen by more than 30 million viewers each week and is broadcast in 110 countries.

In 1987, Oprah established The Oprah Winfrey Foundation to support the education and empowerment of women, children, and families in the United States and around the world. The Oprah Winfrey Scholars Program gives scholarships to students determined to use their education to give back to their communities in the United States and abroad. To date, Oprah's Angel Network, a public charity to impact the lives of others, has raised nearly $20 million for nonprofit organizations around the globe.[5]

It is evident that there is a divine plan, purpose, and destiny for Oprah Winfrey's life, and the world has watched it unfold for two decades. Oprah's selfless commitment and dedication to improving the lives of others is a result of her belief in *I can*.

Who says *you* can't?

7

OVERCOMING THE ODDS

I MAGINE THAT YOUR LIFE is a fingerprint. It is distinctly and uniquely yours. Not only has your life—and all its potential—been assigned to you, but it has also been singled out and designated for a divine purpose. In this life there are no impossibilities. The Book of Life gives us complete assurance that we can do all things; if you can believe it, you can achieve it. How many times have you looked at the circumstances of your life and felt that the odds were stacked against you? We cannot judge our lives by the circumstances or the situation as it appears. We must alter our perception and see things through the eyes of possibility.

It seems that each generation has a new and different set of circumstances that serves to challenge, develop, and mature believers—and nonbelievers alike—into a divine sense of purpose. The generations of our forefathers faced battles of gaining freedom from slavery and oppression from British and foreign rulers. The generation of our parents and grandparents were united in the struggle for peace and equal access to basic human and civil rights. They've shared the memories of a nation torn by warfare and strife, and a nation divided in the pursuit of freedom and equality for all. And many of them still bear the mental and emotional scars of the battles fought.

The historical figures who greatly impacted our society, culture, and world at various times faced tremendously challenging circumstances. I often wonder how many of us could stare impending danger, death, and destruction in the face and confidently proceed toward fulfilling our mission in life. Would we stand steadfastly in the confidence of our faith? Or would we turn and run for safety? What is your response when the odds are greater than your personal strength, power, and resources combined? What is your response when the odds are greater than your faith? Will you still believe that *you can* when it appears there are no options and defeat is imminent?

HELEN KELLER

Helen Keller is probably the most well-known deaf and blind person in recent history. Consider the obstacles she overcame and the level of success she accomplished in her lifetime. There are people walking around today with twenty-twenty vision, perfect hearing, and complete use of their mental faculties, yet they are immobilized by procrastination, excuses, fear, and failure. She overcame unimaginable trials to become a successful author and performer.

WE MUST ALTER OUR PERCEPTION AND SEE THINGS THROUGH THE EYES OF POSSIBILITY.

Most people just know that Helen Keller was deaf and blind and yet able to communicate through a rudimentary form of sign language, grunts, and gestures. But her story is much greater than that. Some of her other accomplishments or notable achievements include the fact that she survived an illness referred to in her day as "brain fever"—a possible form of scarlet fever or meningitis. As an infant, she was given only a short time to live. It was her bout with that illness that caused her complete loss of hearing and sight. Many of us may remember seeing *The Miracle Worker,* a Broadway production and film that recounted her struggle to adjust, learn, and cope with her physical disabilities.

In 1900 Keller enrolled at Radcliffe College and became the first deaf and blind person to ever enroll and graduate from an institution of higher learning, receiving a bachelor of arts and graduating magna cum laude. After graduation, Keller toured the vaudeville circuit and also served as a lecturer for groups around the country that were fascinated by her story and her accomplishments. Several years later, she wrote and published a book called *The Story of My Life*.[1] The film *The Unconquered*, about Keller's life story, went on to win an Academy Award in the mid-1950s. She also received the Presidential Medal of Freedom—the highest civilian award—from President Lyndon B. Johnson in 1964.

Society, medicine, and tradition told Helen Keller, "You can't." But there was one doctor who encouraged her parents not to give up. And there was one teacher by the name of Anne Sullivan who said, "You can." Sullivan taught her student how to fight past the anger, frustration, and bitterness of her condition. She made Keller understand that she was bigger than her circumstances and able to overcome the obstacles if she was willing to try.[2] How many parents during that time would have just given up on a blind and deaf child and sent him or her away to an institution? How many doctors would have looked at the situation and determined it was hopeless?

> THE KEY TO OVERCOMING IS TO GET UP ONE TIME MORE THAN YOU FALL DOWN.

Helen Keller is an excellent example of overcoming staggering physical odds and fulfilling greatness. She's an inspiration to anyone who feels trapped by physical or mental limitations. Helen Keller is a shining example of success.

MOREHOUSE COLLEGE

The Augusta Institute was founded in 1867, two years after the Civil War ended. The school was opened to teach and train newly freed black men in the vocations of education and ministry. What is now Morehouse College in Atlanta, Georgia, began in the basement of Springfield Baptist Church, the oldest independent African American church in the United States.[3]

Over the years, Morehouse has led the nation in educating successful male leaders. If those men of faith could overlook the opposition and the resistance of their time and open a college in the wake of resistance, slavery, and oppression, what excuse do you have for not doing what you've been called to do? If God said you can, who says you can't?

Selfless giving to a cause greater than oneself has always marked individuals of great character. Throughout history we see countless individuals who gave up their own rights to peace and comfort to secure the rights, privileges, and advancement of others.

Today's generations are facing far different challenges than those I've just cited. The current school-aged generation has been called and united to overcome an entirely different set of challenges. Our students face daily threats of terrorism, gang violence, and a morally debase society that worships illicit sex, offensive language, and dishonest conduct. Our young people are being forced to exist and thrive in a world that seeks to decimate and destroy them.

DR. JOHNNETTA B. COLE

In this day and age, we don't have a lot of heroes or heroines. But one particular educator stands out in my mind. Dr. Johnnetta B. Cole is a shining example of commitment to helping others overcome their personal odds and achieve their goals. Dr. Cole's life has been filled with outstanding accomplishments since her youth, but the recurring theme of her life has been her ongoing commitment to educating young people.

AT SOME POINT IN YOUR LIFE, YOU MUST MAKE A COMMITMENT TO DO SOMETHING OF SIGNIFICANCE.

Dr. Cole was born in Jacksonville, Florida, and enrolled at Fisk University at the age of fifteen through the school's early admissions program. She completed her undergraduate degree at Oberlin College and went on to earn master's and doctorate degrees in anthropology from Northwestern University.

Dr. Cole's career as a college and university professor and administrator spans over the course of three decades. She made history in 1987 by becoming the first African American woman to serve as president of Spelman College in Atlanta. At her inauguration as seventh president of Spelman, actor and comedian Bill Cosby—and his wife, Camille—made a gift of $20 million to the school, the largest single gift from individuals to any historically black college or university (HBCU). Under her leadership, Spelman College completed a capital campaign, which raised more than $113.8 million, the largest sum ever raised by an HBCU.

Upon heeding the call from Bennett College in North Carolina—an academic institution in need—Dr. Cole left retirement to lead and restore this valued institution of higher learning. Affectionately known on the Bennett College campus as "Sister President," she is the fourteenth president of Bennett College for Women, which has been a vital source for educating women of color since 1926. Dr. Cole said, "Only the challenge to help Bennett College for Women soar to the height of her possibilities could have lured me out of retirement."

In order to restore Bennett's vitality and reestablish its stellar reputation as a preeminent educational institution for African American women, in June 2003, the Bennett College Board of Trustees launched a $50 million "Revitalizing Bennett Campaign." The funds will be used for student scholarships, faculty recruitment and development, and campus renovations. Former United States Senator Robert "Bob" J. Dole was announced to chair the fund-raising campaign. Under Dr. Cole's leadership, Bennett College was well on its way to being reinstated as a premiere institution of higher education; and one of only two HBCUs for women in the nation.

Both Spelman College and Bennett College have the distinction in history for primarily educating African American women and for being led by Dr. Johnnetta B. Cole. Her legacy with these institutions—as well as the impact the students will make in society—is outstanding. Because of her willingness to nurture the success of others, the entire academic world has benefited.

With more than forty-eight honorary degrees to her credit, Dr. Cole also serves on numerous corporate boards and civic organizations. She is the mother of three sons and a surrogate mother to countless young women in pursuit of higher educational and successful endeavors. Dr. Cole's role as an educator and administrator has been instrumental in the lives of many.[4]

For every graduate of Spelman or Bennett who was told, "You can't," the commitment of Dr. Cole and other educators like her said, "You can." Students who wouldn't be welcome at other institutions are welcomed, warmly embraced, and given the opportunity to pursue greatness and live out their dreams.

Who says you can't get a college education? Who says it's too late to start over? If God didn't say it, then it's just someone else's opinion. At some point in your life, you must make a commitment to do something of significance. It's not important to try to be like someone else; it just matters that you discover the purpose for your life and pursue it with passion.

I challenge you to overcome the odds in your life. I encourage you to defy the difficulties that life may throw your way and commit to succeeding despite the odds. Not too long ago there was an episode about burn victims on television. Some of the individuals featured had been in severe car accidents or fires and had survived only by the grace of God. Many of them were physically burned beyond recognition. The miracle of modern science was able to reconstruct facial features and restore limbs, but it couldn't heal the emotional and mental scars of enduring such a difficult ordeal. That kind of healing only comes from above—and from within.

These survivors overcame the physical damage of smoke inhalation and excessive heat to their skin and organs. They overcame the emotional trauma of not being able to move, hear, or speak with ease. They overcame the disappointment and anger of suffering such tragic occurrences, and they learned how to overlook the stares and snickers from rude and insensitive people. Most importantly, they overcame the sinking feelings of despair and discouragement and the desire to give up and die.

THE NEXT TIME CIRCUMSTANCES WHISPER IN YOUR EAR ABOUT HOW YOU'LL NEVER BE SUCCESSFUL, REMIND YOURSELF ABOUT YOUR DIVINE DESTINY.

Watching the miraculous recoveries over a period of months, and sometimes years, is fascinating to me. I often wonder what kind of faith and resolve one must have in order to overcome such devastating circumstances. But the answer is very clear. We must search inside ourselves to find the intestinal fortitude to believe and hope for the best, no matter what. We must determine that failure is not an option and that we will make it despite the odds. The next time you need to overcome the odds, take inventory of how much power and faith are working inside of you.

How much time do you spend in prayer? How much time do you spend meditating on Scripture and positive affirmations? It is when we are fully committed to fulfilling our divine purpose and walking in our divine destiny that we can expect to see miraculous healing and deliverance from trials and tribulations. Be encouraged that you are an overcomer. Understand that any challenges you encounter can be conquered in the face of your faith. The Bible instructs us to "seek first his kingdom and his righteousness, and all these things will be given to you as well. Therefore do not worry about tomorrow, for tomorrow will worry about itself. Each day has enough trouble of its own" (Matt. 6:33–34).

THE LESSON OF THE UNDERDOG

If you've ever watched sports, then you know that in most competitions, there is always what's called an *underdog.* That's the individual or competitor who shows a lot of heart and tenacity but has little hope of emerging with a victory. Whether it's physical, mental, or financial, the underdog is always in a position of disadvantage and unlikely to win. If he hasn't already lost, the odds are betting that he is going to lose.

In life, many of us feel like the underdog. We feel that our chances of coming out on top are slim to none. We feel that unless something miraculous happens, whatever we're going through will probably take us out of the game. But I want you to know that the heavens are rooting for the underdog. Fate and destiny are cheering on the underdog and telling him how to win. Just know that the key to overcoming is to get up one time more than you fall down. The key to overcoming is to trust that you are never completely alone and that you have not been forgotten. Life has simply selected to strengthen and polish you through your circumstances. The key to overcoming is to consistently and continually believe that *you can.*

Who says you'll always be the underdog? Who says you can't come out on top? It doesn't matter that you failed a grade; just start over and try again. It doesn't matter that you didn't pass the bar exam the first time; hire a tutor, study more, and take it again. It doesn't matter that no one from your family has ever gone to college before. What does that have to do with you? God has designed a successful and prosperous life just for you. It doesn't matter what anyone else says as long as God says, "You can."

> WE MUST DETERMINE THAT FAILURE IS NOT AN OPTION AND THAT WE WILL MAKE IT DESPITE THE ODDS.

What if everybody expects you to fail? What if everybody expects you to give up? What if nobody comes to your rescue? What if nobody lends a helping hand? I want you to know that if God is for you, it's more than the whole world against you. Once you get that in your mind, you will understand the power and significance of faith. Once you realize that no person, adversary, or set of circumstances can hold you back from acquiring what has been purposed for your life, then you can confidently walk into your divine destiny.

The athlete and track star Jesse Owens made history in the 1936 Olympic Games by winning four gold medals—despite all the odds. Even though Owens was a champion athlete at Ohio State University, he was forced to live off campus because of segregation. He faced opposition at every turn, and the odds were stacked against him.

> WE MUST TEACH OUR YOUTH THAT THERE ARE STILL INJUSTICES IN THE WORLD THAT CANNOT BE IGNORED.

Although he was born to a poor family, was treated unfairly, and faced ongoing racism and discrimination, Owens decided that his fate did not rest in the opinions of other people. Because of his accomplishments, he went on to become a successful speaker, spokesman, and role model for countless young athletes. In 1976, he was awarded the Medal of Freedom from President Gerald Ford.[5]

We may not encounter the same obstacles, but the opposition many of us face in our day-to-day lives is just as intense. It's true that our children and grandchildren will never encounter the evils of concentration camps, shackles, and slave ships firsthand. They will never know the devastating impact of legalized prejudice, racism, and discrimination. But they must realize that the world still is not a fair and just place to live. It is imperative they understand that many times in life the odds are stacked against them. We must teach our youth that there are still injustices in the world that cannot be ignored. We must help them to develop compassion for those who are in need.

America is a blessed nation, showered with excess and abundance, while much of the world faces severe need for food, water, and decent shelter. Education and opportunities are not automatic rights and privileges in many regions around the world. The freedom and liberties of democracy are not evident in the eastern part of the globe. In spite of the tremendous strides that have been made here, we cannot turn our backs on the needs of others.

We must instill a sense of pride and accomplishment into our children at an early age because life's negative circumstances would seek to destroy their dreams and their purpose at an early age. Obstacles and challenges come to deceive and discourage us into thinking we cannot overcome the odds, but we are more than conquerors, and we can be eternally victorious in life.

The next time circumstances whisper in your ear about how you'll never be successful or that your future is filled with failure, remind yourself about your divine destiny and assert the God-given authority that's in you to overcome the odds. You are not an underdog. You are not destined for defeat. You are given divine assurance that you can succeed.

You were not put on this earth to "make do" or "barely get by." You were made to rule and to reign. You were called to take dominion and reflect the One in whom you believe. You've seen several examples of people who overcame tremendous odds and accomplished admirable tasks in the face of adversity. The same ability that is in them is in you too.

8

DO NOT WASTE YOUR TRIALS

.

WE ARE ALL GOING to go through trials in life, but don't let anyone scare you with trials. You *will* go through, yet you will also grow as a result of those same trials. We would all like to think that we are on the easy path. We want everything to go "our way" and sail smoothly through the various phases of our journey.

I grew up with six sisters and two brothers. In our neighborhood, whenever some young person was in trouble, that person came to me and expected me to come to their aid. When their parents didn't feed them, I would feed them. When the older ones tried to beat them, I would bring them in. I just loved the kids, and I wanted to be part of this brotherhood. Yet my big brother Eric would be nice to me in the house, but when we got out of the house, he would join in with the rest, and they would punish me. I would run back to my mother and ask, "Why don't they want to play with me?"

My mother would call Eric and tell him, "This is your little brother; you play with him."

He would say, "Mommy, we are going to play with him." But as soon as we were away from her, Eric would do the opposite.

At times I would try to give the neighborhood kids clothes. I would say, "Mommy, the parents will not give them clothes. I believe I could help them." At that time, I didn't know that these attempts to help other kids in the neighborhood were a part of my natural personality traits. I had to grow up before I realized that my love for helping people would later become a part of my ministry, and I learned from it.

> GOD WANTS TO SEE THE CHARACTER THAT YOU WILL DEVELOP IN THE PROCESS OF YOUR TRIAL SO THAT WHEN YOU COME INTO HIS FULL BLESSING, YOU WILL BE ABLE TO SUSTAIN THE BLESSING RATHER THAN LET THE BLESSING DESTROY YOU.

When I was a child, I had my own business. I danced, and people would pay me. I started prospering very early. I was so popular in my town and everywhere around it that when a song melody became a hit, people would singsong my name using the melody. I had a very popular name. Everybody loved me. And when people met me and I told them what my name was, they would make a melody out of it. Now I realize that all these things were preparing me for what I am supposed to be doing today. In some ways, my name has been a blessing in the things I had to face. Yet, there are also ways in which the name has been a curse. But whatever I have been through, it is necessary for what I am doing today. Don't waste your trials!

If you want the anointing of God, you are going to go through trials. If you want financial blessings, you are going to go through trials. If you want a family, you are going to go through trials. Whatever you want, God is going to allow you to go through trials. He will never stop any trial that comes your way, and, actually, sometimes you might think that God has connived with the enemy to bring trials to your life. No! God wants to see the character that you will develop in the process of your trial so that when you come into His full blessing, you will be able to sustain the blessing rather than let the blessing destroy you. Don't waste your trial.

Often we think that trials and temptation begin when you are mature. No, they begin when you are young. Do you realize that our teenagers, our young ones, face more temptations than most adults? The greatest struggles and temptations come to younger people because they are beginning to face the trials and struggles of life. Our children, our young people, know what temptation is all about. They know what struggles are all about.

THE EXAMPLE OF JOSEPH

As we look at Scripture in Genesis, we see the story of Jacob and his descendants. He had many sons, but there was one that he especially loved, Joseph. Joseph's troubles began when he was quite young, at the age of seventeen.

According to the Word of God, even as a teenager Joseph enjoyed work. He was tending his father's flock, and he was attached or committed to his father's business. We are supposed to learn the trade of our fathers. Jesus Christ was the Son of God, and He learned the trade of both His earthly father and His heavenly Father. Throughout His earthly life, His earthly father, Joseph, was a carpenter, and Jesus learned his trade. It is not right for you to call somebody your father when you are not willing to learn his trade. Jesus showed interest in Joseph's work as a carpenter.

> IF YOU DON'T DO WHAT YOU ARE SUPPOSED TO DO AND RESPOND IN THE RIGHT WAY, YOU MAY VERY WELL MISS OUT ON YOUR BLESSING.

But He also showed interest in His heavenly Father's work as a deliverer. If you look at the role of both of His earthly father and His heavenly Father, there are many parallels in what they did. God, our heavenly Father, the King, wants His children back. They left their place in the kingdom, and He wants them back. So Jesus came to bring them back. He came to be the foremost Prince to connect all of us as heirs to the throne.

As a carpenter, He also put things together, this time with wood. Just as He learned to build things with His hands, making the wood with which He worked smoother and putting it together into a new form, so He *builds* in a spiritual sense. If there is something you want put together in your home, just tell Him what you want built, and He will give you something that will be permanent in your home—and the benefit can be generational.

Whenever a carpenter puts a good work together, we often give it to our children as inheritance. It becomes what we call an *antique*, and its value goes up. Whenever God builds your life, puts you together, and attaches you with God, somehow your value goes up.

So, Joseph, as a young, seventeen-year-old man, started about his father's business. One day he had a dream. Wearing the beautiful robe his father had given him, which showed the favoritism Jacob felt for Joseph, Joseph went to his brothers and told them about his dream: "Joseph had a dream, and when he told it to his brothers, they hated him all the more" (Gen. 37:5). That means that they already hated him for being the baby, and they hated him more when he started dreaming. Their hatred became his trial. When he told them the dream, it did not please them.

As we read on, the Bible tells us that he had another dream (v. 9). When he told his father both dreams, his father was not pleased and rebuked him, saying, "What is this dream you had? Will your mother and I and your brothers actually come and bow down to the ground before you?" (v. 10). You see, whatever is important to God, as far as your life is concerned, is the very thing that will get you into trouble. It is the dream that God shows you that will get you in trouble, because every dream has an interpretation. The dream that Joseph had became his trial. But Joseph did not waste his trial. He went through some difficult challenges, and he could have lost it, but he maintained his position to win in the end.

Joseph's brothers became angry with Joseph and jealous of him. His father rebuked him. Your dream will also stir jealousy. The vision that God has for your life will create jealousy. The Bible says that eventually Joseph's brothers sold him to a passing slave trader. That became his trial; he was sold. When God puts a genuine gift in a person's heart, that gift will always find a way to take that person into even deeper troubles until the person learns the things that are necessary for them to know in life.

While you are going through what you need to go through, don't waste your trials. You go through trials in spite of who you are, in spite of what you believe, and in spite of God's plan for your life. Trials are a necessary part of life. Any man or woman born into this world is born into adversity and born to face challenges. Adversity is a necessary part of life.

The response of Joseph's brothers to his divine dream of destiny brought challenges to Joseph. But remember, it was another dream that he had much later, after he had moved into his destiny of authority in Egypt, that saved the lives of the brothers who hated him and sold him into captivity, and the life of the father who had rebuked him. Don't waste your trial. In spite of what you are going through, don't waste it. There are things you have to learn through your trial—you are going to go through some trials, but at the end of the tunnel God has something special for you. So, don't waste your trial!

Joseph was sold into slavery, but because of what he went through, God had actually proven him. He was hated, but he learned how to accept it. His brothers were jealous of him, but he learned how to accept and love them. He was rebuked, which was a normal thing for a father to do because his father's aim of rebuking him was to protect him from his brother's hatred. Yet his brothers caught him in the absence of his father and brought grief to his father.

> YOU GO THROUGH TRIALS IN SPITE OF WHO YOU ARE, IN SPITE OF WHAT YOU BELIEVE, AND IN SPITE OF GOD'S PLAN FOR YOUR LIFE.

Joseph became a young slave in a foreign land, sold by his own brothers. The interesting point about Joseph's slavery, however, is that his love of work and service followed him into slavery. Everything he did, he did with excellence. He did not consider the tasks assigned for him to do to be beneath him, but he considered the outcome of his labors. As a result of his actions, Joseph was noticed by everyone around him, even by the pharaoh. They saw the hand of God on him, and Pharaoh placed him in charge in the midst of all of this.

Don't Miss Out on Your Blessing

There is an important lesson for us to learn through this. Many people have the wrong concept of trials. You may be called to serve someone who is not the person you want to serve. But God is using that person and that place to test your heart to see if you qualify for His blessing by the way you go through your tests. If you don't do what you are supposed to do, and respond in the right way, you may very well miss out on your blessing.

> IT IS ONLY AFTER THE TRIAL HAS PASSED THAT YOU CAN CLEARLY SEE THE WORK THAT HAS BEEN DONE IN YOU.

Joseph brought his God into his trial. He was sold into a foreign country where they worshiped idols and had no value for the one true God. There is a great truth you must learn from this example of Joseph. Joseph did not just work for those who had taken him captive out of a desire to get out of that trial and move on to a greater destiny. He worked for them because that was the place where he found himself, and he was a worker—he was working hard before he was sold, and he didn't lose the ability to work hard when he was in slavery. In spite of his own dream, which seemed lost to him in slavery, his motive remained right, and he worked for his captors to make their own dreams come true.

120

Jesus said that if you make it happen for someone else, God will make it happen for you. In spite of the dream you have, if your dream is not to make somebody's dreams come true, your dream will never come to fruition because your motive will not be right.

If you are lazy in the first place, you will be lazy when you get into trouble. But if you are a worker, wherever you find your place, you will work! If you give excuses before you are sold, you will be giving excuses when you are sold. But if you know that you are a worker no matter what, you feel restless when you don't work. Joseph made sure that in spite of his trial, his attitude toward work was the same. That is why they promoted him. Don't waste your trial. If God is with you when you are going through a trial, He will not leave you in the middle of that trial. He will stay close to you.

Read what happened when Joseph ended up in Potiphar's home:

> Now Joseph had been taken down to Egypt. Potiphar, an Egyptian who was one of Pharaoh's officials, the captain of the guard, bought him from the Ishmaelites who had taken him there. The LORD was with Joseph and he prospered, and he lived in the house of his Egyptian master.
>
> —GENESIS 39:1–2

Joseph was going through a trial that had begun at his own house. Then he was sold to a passing slave trader, who sold him to another person, Potiphar. Yet in all these places, he was being promoted. Joseph was able to look at his trial as a blessing and not a curse. And because he could, God prospered him there in the house of his Egyptian master.

He prospered as a young man because he understood the value of a trial, and he didn't waste it. He was just a teenager, but God was with him as he lived in the house of his Egyptian master. The master, who did not know God, was wise enough to see God's hand on Joseph, because, somehow, when Joseph came to that house, the presence of God came to the house with him.

God will send you through circumstances and situations, but if you do not allow the heart and the Spirit of God to lead you even in that place, you may miss your blessing. Many people have really shipwrecked by looking at things with natural eyes—by sight—and not by the vision God has placed in their hearts.

An important lesson to learn is that our natural eyes see only what is common...ordinary...natural. It takes a person with *vision* to see beyond what is just ordinary. Natural eyes see only ordinary things, but vision sees extraordinary things. You need to have eyes beyond the natural to be able to see. Joseph was seeing the end even though he was a teenager, and the people he served could see the hand of God upon his life. Please don't waste your trials!

BE TRUSTWORTHY IN YOUR TRIAL

The Bible tells us that the Lord was with Joseph in everything and gave him success in everything he did. Joseph found favor in

Potiphar's eyes and became his attendant. Potiphar put every-thing in his care, entrusting to him everything that he owned. From the time he put him in charge of his household and of all that he owned, the Bible tells us that the blessing of the Lord was on everything Potiphar had—both in the house and in the field. So, he left every-thing he had in Joseph's care. He did not concern himself with anything except for what he ate. He trusted Joseph!

NATURAL EYES SEE ONLY ORDINARY THINGS, BUT VISION SEES EXTRAORDINARY THINGS.

Can you be trusted when you go through your trials? I am asking you a question, but don't give me the answer. Let God deal with your heart. Can you be trusted when you are going through your own trials? You can miss the bless-ings of God when your trial is motivated by your own selfishness and you believe you are right and everybody else is wrong.

Please understand that Joseph worked for a man who did not know God, a man who did not call upon Joseph's God. Potiphar was a heathen, yet he received the blessings that Joseph brought into his home. If you are blessed of God, no matter what you do, the blessings follow you, and whatever you touch, the bless-ings of God will flow through you. If you are truly walking as a child of God and are going through trials, the people around you should see the blessings on you from God. The blessings that you bring to them will silence them. However, if you aren't bringing any blessings to them, it is because your complaints and excuses have overtaken what are supposed to be your blessings. Your struggling will increase.

Joseph learned his lessons well and learned them early. The Bible tells us that Jesus Christ learned obedience through the things He suffered (Heb. 5:8). Most of us are not obedient because we have not suffered much. You need to go through some suffering to learn obedience. Out of your suffering God will make a way for you. If you suffer with Him, it is a sign that you are getting ready to reign with Him. Those who suffer with Him shall also reign with Him. (See 2 Timothy 2:12.) The Bible promises that our trials are only momentary and will be far outweighed by the glory that awaits us at the end of the trial. (See 2 Corinthians 4:17.)

> YOU ARE GOING TO BE TRIED, BUT GOD'S INTENTION IS THAT WHEN YOU COME OUT, YOU SHOULD COME OUT LIKE PURE GOLD.

However, if you waste your trial, you will not see the fulfillment of what God desires to bring you into. What do we mean by wasting? We waste our trials by complaining, bickering, and thinking that we deserve better. Joseph could have said that he deserved better, because in his father's house he was favored and only had to attend to his father's flock. But he was forced to mature quickly by the hostile environment into which he was thrust in comparison to where he came from.

You may be about to begin a period of trial in your life. You may have already begun to go through your trials. Try diligently to find a better way to find out the purpose for which you are going through this trial. Don't waste your trial.

Joseph was well built and handsome. That's another trial: your appearance can become your trial. Your height can become your trial. Your slenderness can become your trial. Whatever you are built for, you are built for a trial.

I can tell you from experience that trials are never easy. Like you, I could not decide how I needed to be formed. My height…my weight…I had nothing to do with this. Not even my parents could dictate this; it was all part of God's plan. His Word says that before I was formed in my mother's womb, all my days were ordained by God (Ps. 139:13–16). There was a call upon my life before I was born to be a voice to the nations. God knows what He is doing. Your appearance can attract people and, at the same time, repel other people. No matter how you look, your looks are going to get you into trouble. Many people turn to boxing because others have expressed hatred toward them. They become angry with the world and have to go beat on somebody. Many people in the police force joined because they were tired of being bullied while growing up, and rather than following a call into police work, have decided that is a way to get even with society.

Joseph's build came as a result of his work. His work got him into trouble. Potiphar's wife saw Joseph and wanted something from him that he would not give. When he would not fall into sexual immorality with her, she decided, "I've got to get rid of this young man." So what happened? He got into trouble again. His brothers hated him and sold him to somebody else. He ended up in Potiphar's home and rose to prominence. But once again, no one was there to defend him against her accusations. Yet even through this new trial that brought imprisonment to him, Joseph didn't lose his work ethic. He didn't lose his relationship with God, and even through his trial he didn't curse anyone. He was honoring God in his service. Don't waste your trial.

IF YOU WANT THE ANOINTING OF GOD, YOU ARE GOING TO GO THROUGH TRIALS.

Because God was with Joseph in prison, he prospered even there. It was his *dream* that helped him to be able to interpret dreams. Don't waste your trials. You are going to go through trials in life, if you have not already done so. You are going to be tried, but God's intention is that when you come out, you should come out like pure gold.

It is only after the trial has passed that you can clearly see the work that has been done in you—a work that builds your character, strengthens your resolve, and creates empathy within you to understand the plight of others, making you a better person. Do not waste your trials. You must always strive to understand them and flow with God. In that way, a greater work can be done in your life!

9

TRAGEDY AND TRIUMPH

GREAT ACCOMPLISHMENTS AND MASSIVE success in no way guarantee the absence of obstacles and adversity. In actuality, the price of success is often greater than imagined by those who face the challenge of pursuing greatness.

Anything worth having will cost you something. There is a cost for fear, a cost for failure—and a cost for success. There are devastating losses and astounding victories along the way.

The journey to success is filled with ups and downs, trials and tribulations, doubt and despair, wonder and awe.

It is my belief that without the experiences of difficulty and challenges, we can never fully understand or appreciate the rewards of achievement and accomplishment. Success propels people into the spotlight and places a demand on them that they aren't prepared for. Success often requires that you voice your concerns and convictions in a public manner and then defend your life to all who inquire. Success or celebrity does not exempt anyone from criticism. As a matter of fact, it often magnifies the intensity of the spotlight and the level of scrutiny. Success has ruined many people because the requirements and responsibilities catch them off guard.

> REST ASSURED; WHEN YOUR SUCCESS IS DIVINELY INSPIRED, THERE ARE NO OBSTACLES THAT YOU CANNOT OVERCOME.

But rest assured; when your success is divinely inspired, there are no obstacles that you cannot overcome—and no challenges that cannot be conquered in your life.

Even though he was a man of much controversy, aviator Charles Lindbergh was also a man of great conviction. Although he received much acclaim for making the first nonstop, solo flight across the Atlantic Ocean, Lindbergh was also a political and media lightning rod because of his antiwar sentiments, alleged Nazi Germany ties, acclaimed artificial heart invention,

Pulitzer prize–winning novel, and high-profile kidnapping of his son, Charles Augustus Jr.

For Lindbergh, fame was fast and furious. After his famous 1927 flight, he published *"We,"* a book about his solo transatlantic journey.[1] The title *"We"* referred to Lindbergh and his plane, the *Spirit of St. Louis.* Immediately after he landed, he was thrust into the public spotlight, conducting hundreds of speeches and appearances to talk about aviation and his recent accomplishments. After much controversy, criticism, and acclaim, *"We"* later was awarded the Pulitzer prize in 1954.

Between the years of 1931 and 1934, Lindbergh is credited with inventing an artificial heart for a French surgeon and biologist. Lindbergh's device assisted in pumping the fluids and substances necessary for life throughout various organ tissues.

Lindbergh was honored and revered for his contributions to the medical and aviation industries. But he also drew intense criticism for his vocal campaign against voluntary American involvement in World War II. He was so criticized for what was described as unpatriotic noninvolvement beliefs that he avoided the public spotlight for decades.

Tragedy struck the Lindbergh home in March 1932, when his twenty-month-old son, Charles Jr., was kidnapped. The child's body was found ten weeks after the abduction, and Bruno Hauptmann—a local carpenter—was arrested, tried, and executed for the crime. The news was an international story that caused throngs of reporters, photographers, and curious onlookers to besiege the residence of the Lindbergh family and eventually force them to move to Europe to escape the publicity. However, the kidnapping led to creation of the "Lindbergh Law" legislation, which made kidnapping a federal offense.

In his latter years, Lindbergh developed a deep interest in the cultures of people in Africa and the Philippines. He also pursued activism for the conservation movement and campaigned for ecological interests of endangered species. Although Lindbergh died of cancer in August 1974, his memory and contributions to modern-day aviation, medical devices, and conservation are still evident today. Lindbergh's legacy is still alive and impacting other lives.[2]

We should all strive to leave a living legacy, a path that immortalizes our presence long after we've gone on. What worthwhile endeavors are you pursuing that will live on in your memory? What values are you instilling in your children that will make them contributors to the well-being of this world? What changes are you making in your own life that will positively impact our society? When you're gone, what will people remember you for? How are you making the world a better place?

Sometimes tragedy is the birthplace of triumph. In 1979, five-year-old Laura Lamb became one of the world's youngest quadriplegics when she and her mother Cindi were hit head-on by a repeat drunk-driving offender. Cindi Lamb and some friends joined forces to wage war against drunk drivers everywhere. Less than a year later, thirteen-year-old Cari Lightner was killed by a repeat drunk-driving offender. Lightner and some friends formed MADD—Mothers Against Drunk Drivers, an organization to take action against this type of violence. By the end of 1981, MADD had eleven chapters in four states.[3]

The group's mission is: "To stop drunk driving, support victims of this violent crime and prevent underage drinking." More than twenty years later, MADD now has more than six hundred chapters and Community Action Teams in all fifty states and affiliates in Guam, Canada, and Puerto Rico.[4]

What began as anger and outrage to injustice and tragedy has resulted in countless lives being saved and untold numbers of victims and survivors receiving information, comfort, and support during a difficult and emotional

WHEN YOU'RE GONE, WHAT WILL PEOPLE REMEMBER YOU FOR?

time. MADD has initiated significant changes in legislation and public policy, including the passage of thousands of federal and state anti–drunk driving laws, a victims' bill of rights, crime victim compensation, and national sobriety checkpoint campaigns.

LEARN THIS LESSON: DON'T QUIT

So many times people ask the question, "Why do bad things happen to good people?" There seems to be no easy answer, other than the fact that each and every person has the choice of free will, enabling them to make decisions—good or bad—that result in the respective consequences of their actions. Countless people have blamed or turned away from God because of tragic occurrences that have weakened their faith. But God is the giver of every good and perfect gift from heaven. Yes, God is in complete control and may allow difficult circumstances to occur, but He is neither the creator of confusion nor the source of evil.

Sometimes there are simply inexplicable circumstances that seemingly punish individuals who have done nothing wrong. More than ever, when bad things happen to good people, that is the time to embrace and increase our faith. In many instances, adversity forces us to look deeper into ourselves and find the true source of strength that lies within. Challenges make us look beyond our circumstances and appreciate the true meaning of life and understand what matters most.

Most people are familiar with the incredible and inspirational story of athlete and cancer survivor, Olympic champion and six-time Tour de France winner Lance Armstrong. His triumph over tragedy and compelling biography have inspired millions of individuals.

SOME OF THE MOST UNLIKELY HEROES ARE JUST THAT——UNLIKELY HEROES.

The theme for Armstrong's career is a simple one: despite the odds, don't quit. Although his story is filled with wins, triumphs, championships, and victories, it also has been filled with disappointing defeats, challenges, and unimaginable obstacles. However, the resounding theme of his personal and professional life has been resiliency and tenacity. No matter what the odds or the outcome are, Armstrong is known for picking up the pieces and doggedly pursuing his goals.

Like so many others, he has had plenty of opportunities to make excuses and find reasons to fail. He was raised by a single parent, almost didn't graduate from high school, and placed dead last in his first high-profile professional race. Determined not to quit, and encouraged to keep going by his mother, Armstrong kept practicing, kept training, and prepared himself for the next race. By the next season, he acquired ten titles and took his first stage victory in the prestigious Tour de France, and became the youngest road-racing world champion ever.

But just when it seemed that there was nowhere to go but up, tragedy struck. Armstrong was diagnosed with testicular cancer, which had also spread to his lungs and brains. He underwent two surgeries to remove the cancer and then underwent intensive, aggressive chemotherapy treatment. The chemotherapy worked, and he began riding and training only five months after his diagnosis. On many occasions, Armstrong has been quoted as saying, "Getting cancer was the best thing that ever happened to me." In interviews, he says that the illness and subsequent recovery process forced him to change his priorities and appreciate the blessings of good health, a loving family, and close friends. He describes his bout with cancer as a "special wake-up call." He celebrated his victory over cancer by returning to racing and reemerging as a champion.

Armstrong is now a spokesman for testicular and other forms of cancer. He also started the Lance Armstrong Foundation, an international nonprofit to benefit cancer research and promote cancer awareness.[5]

Were there times in your life when it appeared that you were down for the count? What excuses have you made for not accomplishing your goals? Who says you can't have your heart's desires? Who says you can't overcome obstacles? Who says you can't accomplish your goals? Who says you won't recover? Who says you'll never succeed? If God didn't say it, then it's just someone else's opinion.

SUCCESS TAKES DETERMINATION AND COMMITMENT

What amazes me most is the undeniable commitment and determination of individuals who seem to have everything going against them. There are so many stories and examples of individuals who should have failed—but simply had the desire to succeed. It appears that the greater the odds against them, the greater their determination to overcome them. On any given day, we hear stories of victims, survivors, immigrants, and orphans who left behind unimaginable hardship with nothing more than the clothes on their back and a dream in their heart. Their stories educate, motivate, and inspire others to greatness. Some of the most unlikely heroes are just that—unlikely heroes.

Cesar Chavez is by far one of America's most famous and well-respected Hispanic leaders. He was born in Yuma, Arizona, in 1927. During the Depression of the 1930s, his family became victims of tough economic times and dishonest landowners.

The family lost their farm and was forced into migrant farm work to survive. Most of the time, they lived in overcrowded quarters that had no running water, electricity, or bathrooms. They sometimes slept in their car. For years, Chavez attended school and worked in the fields to help provide for his family. Due to the frequent moves, he attended more than thirty schools and only graduated from the eighth grade. He then became a full-time migrant worker.

At age seventeen, Chavez joined the U.S. Navy to better provide for his family. He served two years and returned to San Jose, California, where he began working for the Community Service Organization to help with voter registration and battle economic discrimination against farm workers.

> THERE IS HOPE IN KNOWING THAT GOD IS STILL IN CONTROL AND THAT HE LOVES EACH AND EVERY ONE OF US UNCONDITIONALLY.

In 1962, Chavez and Dolores Huerta founded the National Farm Workers Association, which later became the United Farm Workers (UFW).

Chavez modeled an undying commitment to the cause of improving life and opportunities for poor, struggling farm workers. Through his tireless and nonviolent protests and action, he helped build the UFW into a dues-paying organization with more than fifty thousand members. It was evident on many occasions that he was willing to sacrifice his life to further the cause of the UFW. In 1968, he went on a water-only fast that lasted for twenty-five days. He repeated the fast in 1972 for twenty-four days, and then again in 1988 for thirty-six days. Entertainers and political and civic leaders alike picked up where Chavez left off to champion the cause of farm workers. Rev. Jesse Jackson, Kerry Kennedy, Carly Simon, and actors Martin Sheen, Emilio Estevez, Julie Carmen, Danny Glover, and Whoopi Goldberg also participated in the 1988 fast.

For more than three decades, Chavez led the first successful farm workers union in American history, achieving dignity, respect, fair wages, medical coverage, pension benefits, and humane living conditions for hundreds of thousands of farm workers. He also led successful nonviolent boycotts and strikes that resulted in the first industry-wide labor contracts in the history of American agriculture. His union's efforts brought about the passage of the 1975 California Agricultural Labor Relations Act to protect farm workers. Today, it remains the only law in the nation that protects the rights of farm workers to unionize.

In 1993, Chavez died peacefully in his sleep, not far from his birthplace of Yuma, Arizona—sixty-six years before. Those he helped, encouraged, and led in life also honored him in death. More than fifty-thousand mourners came to honor his life and legacy. His funeral was the largest of any labor leader in the United States. On August 8, 1994, his widow, Helen Chavez, accepted the Medal of Freedom from President Clinton on his behalf. The president honored his memory for having "faced formidable, often violent opposition with dignity and nonviolence." His motto in life was, "Si se puede" (it can be done).[6]

In 2003, Chavez was honored as a civil rights leader on a U.S. postage stamp. The stamp's image portrays a portrait of Chavez against a background of empty grape fields. The following text appears on the back of the stamp: "Civil rights leader Cesar E. Chavez (1927–1993) founded the United Farm Workers of America, AFL-CIO. A tireless advocate for justice and equality for all people, he dedicated his life to working in service of others."[7]

BATTLE SCARS

Sometimes the battle scars from the challenges we face in life follow us forever. Not all the reminders of pain and tragedy can be removed or erased from our memories. However, we serve a God who is able to heal every hurt, remove every sorrow, and work all things in our lives for our good. Maybe someone mistreated you and hurt you. Maybe you were wronged and given a raw deal. Maybe you were needlessly victimized. You don't have to be a victim forever. With God's help, you can pick up the pieces and start all over again. Who says you can't?

> SOMETIMES THE BATTLE SCARS FROM THE CHALLENGES WE FACE IN LIFE FOLLOW US FOREVER.

It's not too late to start over again. It's not too late to make a difference. It's not too late to achieve your dreams. It's not too late to make a positive change. Who says you can't? If God didn't say it, then it's just someone else's opinion.

Tanisha Bagley is a survivor of domestic violence, and also the author of a book titled, *The Price of Love*.[8] For more than eleven years—beginning at age fourteen—she endured physical, sexual, emotional, financial, and mental abuse from her boyfriend and future husband.

Used with her permission, here is the introduction to her book:

> Every now and then a cold sweat wakes me up in the middle of the night. I sit up gasping for air with my arms over my head—trying to protect myself from an invisible assailant like the one that had victimized me for the past 15 years. The sound of my own heartbeat drumming in my chest only intensifies the fear I feel. Instinctively, I run to my children's bedrooms to make sure they're OK. They are. The three of them are sleeping peacefully under the down comforters and bedspreads they got last Christmas. For them, the world is a safe place.
>
> I survey each room, and they're all empty. But the fear is still there. It never goes away. As I try to close my eyes and fall back into wakeful fits of sleep, I can find no comfort. There is never any peace in knowing that somewhere he's still out there. Even my daydreams are filled with anguish and the memory of a man who for years beat me mercilessly. The scars

and bruises on my body have long-since healed, but the lacerations on my heart and mind are beyond repair.[9]

Like most young girls, Bagley had her whole life ahead of her and was looking forward to making new friends, going to the prom, and graduating from high school. She then planned on going to college and having a successful career. At age fourteen, she met her boyfriend and future husband, who ultimately would be arrested and sent to prison for kidnapping and raping her.

Growing up in a household with three generations, Bagley witnessed a lot at an early age. Both her mother and grandmother suffered at the hands of an abuser and were victimized by domestic violence. Bagley decided that her life would be different. Unfortunately, she encountered a similar set of circumstances that were designed to derail her life.

ANYTHING WORTH HAVING WILL COST YOU SOMETHING.

She describes the first few months of her relationship as "wonderful." She and her boyfriend became best friends and spent an overwhelming amount of time together—falling in love. In her mind, he was charming, intelligent, and polite. He was her real-life Prince Charming, and she felt like the luckiest girl in the world. Throughout her high school years, her boyfriend abused her, and he became increasingly violent throughout the duration of their relationship.

When he left for college, she figured that the abuse would end and she would have a chance to recapture the youth that had escaped her. But his controlling anger and abusive behavior only increased. Bagley's boyfriend constantly called, threatened her, and traveled home every weekend to monitor and control her activities. If he didn't like her clothes or the people she was spending time with, he would punch, slap, kick, or beat her as punishment. Her life was terrorized with fear and intimidation.

Bagley got pregnant several times and endured a miscarriage during her high school and young adult years. On what should have been the happiest day of her life—her wedding day—she and her husband got into an argument, and he hit her in the car on the way to their honeymoon destination. For months, the young couple struggled for money and struggled to make ends meet. To help provide for her family, she worked two full-time jobs during her pregnancy and eventually stole money from an employer. She was arrested and found guilty for felony embezzlement. That was the first crime she had ever committed; she no longer recognized herself.

Bagley saw her entire life spiraling out of control. When her husband began routinely beating her in front of their children and telling them to tease and disrespect her, she knew it was time to get out.

After filing charges against her husband and securing a police restraint and protective order, it appeared that the nightmare was ending. But the worst was yet to come. Bagley's husband showed up at her job, hid in the trunk of her car, and kidnapped her. He took her to an abandoned warehouse and sexually assaulted her. At the trial, he was found guilty of sexual assault, second-degree rape, and felonious restraint, and then sentenced to five years in prison.[10]

After the trial, the judge gave Bagley an opportunity to speak. This is the message she shared:

> All I can say is that I'm sorry; I'm sorry that it had to come to this. I hate it for my kids mainly, because of their relationship with their father. And like I said in my testimony, my kids were the main reason I stayed with him. It's tough to raise three children alone, but I'm doing it. I've been doing it alone, and I'll continue to do it alone. This may sound harsh, but as far as I'm concerned, he's the one who made the decision to not be a part of his kids' lives when he did what he did to me. I've done everything I can do for this man. I have been with him for so long, and I've put up with so much stuff that nobody knows about. I used to feel really guilty and like somehow things were my fault. And even though he did horrible, horrible things to me, I forgave him anyway because I loved him. But I think I'm finally coming to the point that I realize he has to take responsibility for his own actions. I'm just sorry that it came to this, and I'm really sorry that he didn't try to get the help he needed. I just wish he would have listened—if not to me, to somebody.

I want to apologize to my children, because I know how much we hurt them. I wish that things could have been different. I'm sorry they had to witness the violence and abuse in our home, and I'm sorry they had to grow up so fast and deal with adult issues—even though they're still so young. I love my children more than anything in this world, and I would do anything to protect them. I'm just glad that this nightmare has finally come to an end.

To the reporters covering this trial, I'd like them to let the world know that domestic violence is real, and it's a serious issue facing this nation. Women all over this country are prisoners in their own homes. It's up to you to educate your readers and listeners about domestic violence.

I want to thank everyone who testified in this trial on my behalf and tell everyone who stood by my side how much I appreciate them. There were days when I thought I wasn't going to make it. There were days when I didn't want to wake up and face another day. I didn't want to become a statistic. I didn't want to be divorced. I didn't want my children to grow up without their father. I didn't want to become a single mother raising three children by myself. And I definitely didn't want to send another young man to prison. But this is the hand that [has been] dealt to me, and I'm playing it every day.

I'm a fighter. And today, I'm a winner. That's all I have to say."[11]

Today, Bagley is an author, public speaker, entrepreneur, and advocate for victims and survivors of domestic violence. She is also the founder of ENSHRINE (Everyone Needs Support, Help, Respect, Inspiration, Nourishment, and Empowerment), a nonprofit organization that provides safe housing, financial support, job training, mentoring, and counseling for women and children who have been victimized by domestic abuse and violence.

> ADVERSITY FORCES US TO LOOK DEEPER INTO OURSELVES AND FIND THE TRUE SOURCE OF STRENGTH THAT LIES WITHIN.

Her personal testimony (as a survivor of domestic violence) has inspired audiences across the country. Her real-life story of tragedy and triumph is featured in a documentary titled *Something So Beautiful*—available from Interact, a safety support and awareness agency for individuals impacted by domestic violence.[12]

Bagley is a mother of three and enjoys spending time with her children, enjoying nature, and watching her favorite movies.

NO ONE IS IMMUNE TO HARDSHIP

In this day and age, it seems that no one is immune to hardship. To quote Allen Patterson, a young man who has faced his share of adversity, "troubles are universal."

Patterson was a nineteen-year-old athlete and college soph-
omore when senseless tragedy struck and forever altered his
life. In 1995, while visiting the nation's capital with several
friends, Patterson was victimized by a random highway drive-
by shooting.

Eleven bullets hit the car he was riding in, and the first bullet
struck him in the neck, inches away from his cervical verte-
brae. The emergency room doctors said that he wouldn't live
through the night. He suffered a C2 spinal cord injury that left
him paralyzed from the chest down, an injury similar to that of
Hollywood actor Christopher Reeves, whom Patterson met at a
rehabilitation facility during his recovery process.

Nine years later, he was still confined to a wheelchair and
needed a respirator to help him breathe. Initially, he had no
movement or sensory functions at all below his neck. He later
regained slight movement in both arms and his right leg (a
medical miracle), but most importantly, he had an unshakable
confidence and faith that he would experience a full recovery
and walk again.

Patterson used these tragic circumstances to inspire others
to overcome the obstacles in their lives. He was featured on
Good Morning, America, and also spoke to various groups
and organizations to educate them about spinal cord injuries.
Patterson returned to school to pursue his business degree. He
also started a nonprofit corporation, Patterson Outreach Minis-
tries, to deliver messages of hope and inspiration to others. He
is now deceased, but his story is still an inspiration.

So, when things appear to be at their absolute worst, how can you still make the best out of a bad situation? Where do we find the inspiration to keep going when it seems that everything around us is falling apart? How do we find the desire to succeed when the odds seem insurmountable? How do we react when trouble finds us and singles us out? There is hope in knowing that God is still in control and that He loves each and every one of us unconditionally.

REMEMBER, IF *GOD* SAID YOU CAN, THEN WHO SAYS YOU CAN'T?

Each one of the individuals mentioned faced some type of tragedy, yet demonstrated a triumphant victory over their circumstances. Each of them is an inspiration in their own right, and each of them deserves all the success that life has to offer. All over this nation and all over this world, people from all walks of life are staring adversity in the face and refusing to accept anything less than the fulfillment of their hopes and dreams.

Allow these stories of real-life heroes to inspire you and propel you toward greatness. Who says you can't be victorious over your circumstances? Who says you can't accomplish your goals? Who says you'll never succeed? Who says you can't have it all? If God didn't say it, then it's just someone else's opinion.

10

STAYING FOCUSED

GETTING AND STAYING FOCUSED on the right things is not just a challenge we face, but in our frenzied world today, it has become a genuine societal concern. Either we find ourselves not being focused at all, or we find ourselves focusing on the wrong things. As long as we live in an era where we are expected to do more—in less time—staying focused becomes crucial to our success.

Like most of you, getting and staying focused is a relentless challenge for me also. I have responsibilities for oversight in so many areas. With proper focus I can impact not only my own future but also the lives of multitudes of people in the United States, in Africa, and in other nations where I speak. Over the years, I have had to learn to improve my mental focus by enhancing my decision-making ability. Let's face it—as long as we're asked to do more in less time, we will always have a problem trying to *get focused*.

WE MUST TAKE GREAT CARE NOT TO GET CAUGHT UP IN ATTACKS OF THE ENEMY THAT WOULD DIVERT US FROM OUR PREASSIGNED GOALS.

Paul addressed these issues in his day as well in his letters to the Philippian church.

> Finally, brothers, whatever is true, whatever is noble, whatever is right, whatever is pure, whatever is lovely, whatever is admirable—if anything is excellent or praiseworthy—*think about such things.*
> —PHILIPPIANS 4:8, EMPHASIS ADDED

Essentially he was telling them to *stay focused.* He had just told them in earlier verses to "stand firm in the Lord" (v. 1), to "not be anxious about anything" (v. 6), and that "the peace of God, which transcends all understanding, will guard your hearts and your minds in Christ Jesus" (v. 7).

With the ease of access to information via cable networks and satellite TV, we can readily identify with an Olympic athlete competing for the ultimate prize. We await with eagerness the release of the gun signifying the beginning of a race. If you watch the faces of the competitors as they ready themselves for takeoff, you see the supreme degree of focus. They do not see or hear anything around them with the exception of the explosion of that gun. They are sharp, at attention, and concentrating on a clearly definable objective. If they take their mind off the goal for one moment, they may miss the mark. The years of preparation and training can be cast off with a single fleeting distraction.

We can easily spend valuable time and energy on projects that have nothing to do with our ultimate goal and/or vision. It is often referred to as *majoring in the minors*. We must take great care not to get caught up in attacks of the enemy that would divert us from our preassigned goals. Many times God's plan for us is to go from point A to point B, but because of disregard for His Word, insensitivity to the Holy Spirit, or not actually discerning the seasons and timing in which we live in, we end up walking away from God's plans and process.

It is possible to be in the wilderness for such a long time that by the time you get to where you're supposed to be, you've lost energy and are unable to enjoy what God has given you. What is the benefit of getting all the accolades in the world and yet have no strength or energy to enjoy it? It can all become useless. Solomon called it *vanity* and said it all comes to naught. But when God gives you grace to enjoy what He's blessed you with, your light shines before men, and they give glory to your God.

It is amazing how God so badly wants us to receive His blessing, and yet we struggle so hard to miss it. God brought the children of Israel out of Egypt, delivered them, and protected them, but He did not tell them they would not have any trou-

bles. God didn't tell them they would have no challenges. It is foolish to believe that when you become a believer, you never face challenges.

WHAT IS THE BENEFIT OF GETTING ALL THE ACCOLADES IN THE WORLD AND YET HAVE NO STRENGTH OR ENERGY TO ENJOY IT?

The Bible tells us clearly that if you really want to see a person who is righteous, look at what a person goes through. The Bible says: "Many are the afflictions of the righteous, but the LORD delivers him out of them all" (Ps. 34:19, NKJV). The Bible does not say that being righteous will

mean that *you always* stand, for it says: "For though a righteous man falls seven times, he rises again, but the wicked are brought down by calamity" (Prov. 24:16). God knows how to deliver His own. When you recognize that "the one who is in you is greater than the one who is in the world" (1 John 4:4), you can operate in strength and in power!

The people of Israel were brought out of bondage, but God told them, "My children, you are going to face some enemies. The very land I'm going to give you is surrounded by enemies. They will keep you from entering into the land. You may have to fight your way through to possess the land that belongs to you." There are times you have to fight your way through to get hold of what is ahead of you.

As we look at Scripture, we can see men and women who were able to take God at His Word and live through distractions, interruptions, delays, detours, oppositions, resistance, insults, criticism, and pressure, and how they succeeded. We can learn, by example, from those who lost their focus and wavered off their path.

In Genesis chapter 3, we see the beginning of a man losing focus, and we can see what has happened as a result to us as a people.

> Now the serpent was more crafty than any of the wild animals the LORD God had made. He said to the woman, "Did God really say, 'You must not eat from any tree in the garden'?" The woman said to the serpent, "We may eat fruit from the trees in the garden, but God did say, 'You must not eat fruit from the tree that is in the middle of the garden, and you must not touch it, or you will die.'"
>
> —GENESIS 3:1–3

The enemy distracted Eve to the point that she distorted or slanted the truth. God didn't say to them, "If you touch the tree, you will die"; He just said, "Don't eat it." But because the enemy distracted her, she went one step further. Remember that in your life, once you are distracted, you go further than you're supposed to go.

In verse 4–6 we see, "'You will not surely die,' the serpent said to the woman. 'For God knows that when you eat of it your eyes will be opened, and you will be like God, knowing good and evil.' When the woman saw that the fruit of the tree was good for food and pleasing to the eye, and also desirable for gaining wisdom, she took some and ate it."

> IF YOU LOSE YOUR FOCUS, YOU HAVE GIVEN IN TO THE ENEMY.

No man can give you something that is beyond God's ability to give you. Whatever you can receive from man, God can give you better. "Every good and perfect gift is from above, coming down from the Father of the heavenly lights, who does not change like shifting shadows" (James 1:17). Man can give you gifts, but his gifts are not perfect. Man's gifts are connected to or given with motives.

Do Not Become Distracted

After Adam and Eve sinned and were sent out of the garden, the day came that God decided, "OK, I'll clean up the earth and wipe man off the face of the earth." (See Genesis 6.) God looked around until He found Noah, who had found favor in the sight of God. God told Noah, "I'm going to bring forth a flood that will clean out the earth, but before that is done, I want you to build Me an ark."

God gave him the dimensions, and Noah took them, and he stayed focused. Many people came and asked him, "Noah, what are you doing?" Whenever God gives you a task to do, there are those who can try to distract you.

There are certain distractions that need to be accepted. God may send distractions to keep you from destruction. However, when you are in the right path—following your purpose, your mission—you will not allow distractions to be a factor in your life.

If you lose your focus, you have given in to the enemy. If you lose your focus, you will speak doubt and unbelief. You will speak fear, and you will not even walk in faith. Many believers today don't walk in faith; they live by fate rather than faith. They go to church, they pray, but they do not exercise faith in God at all. If you are focused on the Word of God when distraction comes, you will still maintain because you know what God told you.

There is an important lesson we can learn from the third chapter of Acts. Verse 1 says, "One day Peter and John were going up to the temple at the time of prayer—at three in the afternoon." The King James Version says, "...being the ninth hour." It was three o'clock in the afternoon. What men are found praying around three o'clock in the afternoon? Most people will pray early in the morning or at night. If men are praying at three in the afternoon, *they are committed to prayer.* They have focus and determination; they want to accomplish something.

The Bible continues by saying:

Now a man crippled from birth was being carried to the temple gate called Beautiful, where he was put every day to beg from those going into the temple courts. When he saw Peter and John about to enter, he asked them for money. Peter looked straight at him, as did John. Then Peter said, "Look at us!"

—ACTS 3:2–4

The man was begging for money. They had seen him there many times before and were aware of his condition. The man was trying to solve his immediate problem, which was money, but Peter and John did something unique. Peter looked at him said, "Look at us." He was already looking at them, but when they said, "Look at us," they took his attention off the money he was thinking about and put his attention on their words. Suddenly the man focused his attention on Peter and John. Peter wanted to get the man's undivided attention. He went on to say, "Silver or gold I do not have, but what I have I give you. In the name of Jesus Christ of Nazareth, walk" (v. 6).

> NO MAN CAN GIVE YOU SOMETHING THAT IS BEYOND GOD'S ABILITY TO GIVE YOU.

That statement reinforced the man's focus because he heard something for the very first time that pricked his heart. Then Peter took him by the hand, and he stood on his feet. This time the man was no longer begging—now he joined them in praising God. They went into the temple, and he started leaping, jumping, dancing, and praising God. He had given Peter his undivided attention, and a miracle had been accomplished as a result of that contact.

Maintaining your focus is very important. Distractions will always come, and when you get distracted, you can easily forget what God told you. It's much like a small child to whom you give a toy. That child will play with the toy until you give him another toy. Then the child forgets the toy he's playing with and becomes fascinated with the new one that has just come on the scene. There are so many people who are just playing with toys. They have lost focus; they don't know what they want, so all they want is God to give them "toys," and they are living life as if everything is bought from the store.

LIVE YOUR LIFE BY THE WORD OF GOD

I am often amazed by some in the body of Christ. Every year a new fad comes out. There may be a new word or terminology that catches everyone's attention. It becomes so overused that they then start with other new words. Everyone is talking about the same things because it's the latest word to use. It is no longer revelation but the latest fad. We live rather by what is in, and what is in always goes out of fashion just as quickly. The Word of the Lord was there before the foundation of the world, and it never goes out of fashion!

> Let your eyes look straight ahead,
>   fix your gaze directly before you.
> Make level paths for your feet

and take only ways that are firm.
Do not swerve to the right or the left;
keep your foot from evil.

—PROVERBS 4:25–27

No matter how long it takes, hold on to the Word of the Lord; God will not fail! "God is not a man, that he should lie, nor a son of man, that he should change his mind. Does he speak and then not act? Does he promise and not fulfill?" (Num. 23:19).

> NO MATTER HOW LONG IT TAKES, HOLD ON TO THE WORD OF THE LORD; GOD WILL NOT FAIL!

Additionally, don't allow yourself to despise the days of small beginnings. Small beginnings will give you good mileage in the years to come. Learn to rest in God and trust in His Word. The Bible says, "A thousand may fall at your side, ten thousand at your right hand, but it will not come near you" (Ps. 91:7). It also affirms, "You will only observe with your eyes and see the punishment of the wicked" (v. 8).

When I started in life, do you know what people said I couldn't do? Do you know those who laughed at me and the oppositions I went through? If I looked at people, I would think God has failed. But when I look at God, I see His plans for me.

> Let us draw near to God with a sincere heart in full assurance of faith, having our hearts sprinkled to cleanse us from a guilty conscience and having our bodies washed

156

with pure water. Let us hold unswervingly to the hope
we profess, for he who promised is faithful.

—HEBREWS 10:22–23

As you read that verse, remember that attacks come to keep
you in touch with God and attached to God.

THE RESULTS OF BEING UNFOCUSED

When you are not focused, many things happen to you. I want
to give you six things that will happen to you when you are not
focused.

1. Whenever you feel intimidated and insecure, it's
   because you are not focusing on God. If you have
   not put your mind on the Lord, your mind is off
   the Lord; you are wavering or swerving, you are
   not keeping focus. When a person is not focused,
   they are double minded. If you are not focused,
   you become *double minded.*

2. When you are not focused, you will live a life of
   confusion.

3. Without focus, you will live a life of doubt and
   fear.

4. Without focus, you are unstable.

5. Without focus, you will be filled with anxiety.

6. Unless you maintain your focus, you will live a
   life of failure.

THE RESULTS OF FOCUS

Now let us take a look at what occurs when you *stay focused*! There are seven things that happen to you when you are focused.

1. God will lead you in all of your ways.

2. God will strengthen you. You will have strength, and nothing will move you.

3. When you're focused, you will have rest.

4. Your soul will be at peace.

5. When you are focused, you will have hope.

6. You will have faith to accomplish great things.

7. When you are focused, you will succeed.

Don't limit yourself by looking at your life in only one aspect. View your life in its completion, and see your life as the spirit man and soul in the body. When you see yourself in that light, you will be able to apply the Word of God to every area of your life. When God talks about blessing, He is not talking about just material blessing. He is talking about blessing us spiritually, physically, emotionally, financially, and socially. When God talks about healing, He will heal you spiritually but also physically and emotionally. When

> STAY FOCUSED, AND YOU WILL SEE SUCCESS AS HE COMPLETES HIS WORK IN YOU!

God talks about protection, He means spiritual and physical as well. So whatever God says in His Word, apply it to every area of your life.

11

DIVINE DELAY IS A
BLESSING IN DISGUISE

WE LIVE IN A microwave society where we expect immediate service in all aspects of life. We have fast-food restaurants where we drive through for our meals, becoming impatient for even slight delays on our morning coffee run. We have our BlackBerrys in full operation, giving us immediate access to the Internet, and we are able to speak to people in all time zones, day or night. Everybody wants it *now*, wants it fast, and when we get less-than-stellar quality because of the corners cut in rushing it us, we complain that no one is paying attention to *us* and our needs!

We look for ways to speed up our lives—with picture-in-picture TV, automatic commercial skip, automatic teller machines at our drive-through banks as we map our way on our high-tech GPS systems. We chat, we blog, we text, we video-conference. And when everything is in such a hurry, we totally lose patience for the age-old art of *delay*! The concept of a "delayed blessing" becomes more and more difficult to understand.

Many of you can honestly say that there were times when you felt that your blessings had been delayed. You prayed; you believed the Lord. You did what you thought was right. You reminded yourself of God's Word and said, "I know my God can do it," and yet you didn't see the answer.

Like you, I have felt this way many times. I have believed God. Usually when I feel the presence of God, I just believe that before I even open my eyes, it will be done! But there have been times when I opened my eyes and realized that *it is not done.* Then I continue in faith, reminding myself of His Word, and saying, "I know that although it didn't happen right at this moment, it's going to happen tomorrow...or it's going to happen in two weeks." Sometimes it goes well beyond the two weeks. Somehow I seem to forget that I have prayed, and all of a sudden, at the appointed time, here comes an answer without my struggling or worrying myself about it.

I believe that there are also instances where we have prayed, yet we hardly feel the presence of God. It may actually take you a long time to get the words out of your heart, or out of your mouth, and when they do come out, it may seem that they didn't even come out right.

You must understand that in the times when you pray eloquently, just because you believe *and feel* that God has absolutely heard you, that doesn't mean that He will answer immediately.

Or there may be other times when you get before God and you have so much in your heart and mind that you just don't know where to start. You may start praying and suddenly a thought comes into your mind that you think you should say first, and your words are just all mixed up. I know that this has happened to me, and it often seems that it is at those times when I think I am least coherent that God seems to answer my prayers.

> THERE ARE CERTAIN TIMES WHEN GOD WILL NOT DO THINGS AS YOU EXPECT SO THAT YOUR FAITH WILL NOT REST IN WHAT YOU SAY BUT IN WHAT HE SAYS!

When that happens, I tend to ask myself, "Why didn't God answer my prayer when I was high in the Spirit? Why did He answer when I seemed least in tune with Him?" God will then remind me, "You only thought you were high in the Spirit. You were just very impressed with the words that were coming out of your mouth." In those defining moments,

God always seems to encourage me that it is not by might, it is not by power, *it is by His Spirit!*

I want to submit to you that divine delay is often a blessing in disguise. There are certain times God allows things to take place to prepare us for something great. If we understand that, we will not be anxious but will rest in God. We will smile when we are normally tempted to get nervous. When we know that divine delay is a blessing in disguise, we will not worry our minds or disturb our sleep but will rather lean on Him.

A FAMILY WHO LEARNED THE IMPORTANCE OF DIVINE DELAY

There is a man in the Bible who had a relationship with Jesus Christ. Not only this brother but his sisters also had relationships with Jesus. We read in John chapter 11 that Lazarus, Mary, and Martha had established a close friendship with Jesus. They were able to fellowship with the most important person who has ever lived and walked the face of the earth. Their close friend was God revealed in the flesh.

Who wouldn't want to be around Jesus? The Bible tells us that the throngs wanted to get close to Him whenever He was nearby. In fact, His disciples loved being so close to Him that they felt they had the most important job in the world. They tried to protect Him from people—don't touch Him, leave Him alone. They even tried to scare children away from Him.

Yet, because of His close friendship with Mary, Martha, and Lazarus, even in the midst of His busy schedule, He would go and sit in their home and eat and talk with them. He genuinely loved them and enjoyed visiting with them from time to time.

However, one day Lazarus became ill, and word came to Jesusthat His friend was very sick, very sick. He did not move.... He waited. He delayed. Now, if we are friends and I am in need of you and call upon you, you would do every-thing possible to help me. The Bible talks about friendship being even deeper than blood. Friendship is a bond that is even stronger than biological ties. You will do everything for a friend. That's the kind of friend Jesus is to us. The reason why we can boldly come to Jesus is not

> THE REASON WHY WE CAN BOLDLY COME TO JESUS IS NOT BECAUSE HE IS OUR BROTHER. THE MOST IMPORTANT THING IS THAT HE IS OUR FRIEND.

because He is our brother. The most important thing is that He is our friend. He is a friend who sticks closer than a brother (Prov. 18:24). He said, after all, "You are my friends if you do what I command. I no longer call you servants... Instead, I have called you friends" (John 15:14–15).

Mary and Martha were concerned about their brother's illness, and yet Jesus did not move. He stayed in one place until His friend died. Mary and Martha felt that Jesus should have showed up when they called for help. After all, He had been healing everyone, raising the dead; but now this is His close friend, and Jesus tarried.

Why didn't Jesus go when He heard that Lazarus was ill? He delayed.

If a friend calls you and says, "My house is on fire," what will you do? You will jump out of bed. You don't care if you come out of the house in pajamas or without pajamas, because in crises something within you tends to violate natural laws. In crises you can get out of the house and never consider that it is winter. In crises you can abuse the natural laws around you as there is something within you that tells you, "My friend needs me, and I have to go to his rescue."

> IT IS TRUE THAT WHEN *YOU* CAN'T DO IT, THERE IS ONE WHO CAN DO IT, AND HIS NAME IS JESUS.

That's what God expects even out of believers. We have to be so close as friends that when a brother or sister needs you, they don't normally have to call you twice. You have to get up! My friend needs me. He is my brother but also my friend. My sister needs me, and she is my friend. She needs me, and I have to get up and go.

But look at Jesus; He delayed. He didn't get up; He didn't jump. He told the disciples, "Our friend Lazarus is sleeping." They said, "Oh, that is good—at least he is sleeping." They may have thought, "Yeah, he's sleeping when we are working."

But Jesus told them, "You don't understand. He is dead." But yet, Jesus stayed in one spot.

I can almost feel what Mary and Martha were feeling. "Oh,

Jesus, our friend. He goes all over the world. He heals everyone. But He's not coming here to respond to us when we need Him the most." They kept the body of the brother for four days. Finally, Jesus decided to go there.

I want you to see something here in John 11, verse 17: "On his arrival, Jesus found that Lazarus had already been in the tomb for four days." The Bible goes on to say, "Bethany was less than two miles from Jerusalem, and many Jews had come to Martha and Mary to comfort them in the loss of their brother. When Martha heard that Jesus was coming, she went out to meet him, but Mary stayed at home" (vv. 18–20).

I understand why Mary stayed at home. I believe that Mary felt that He had failed them, and she was upset with Him. She was thinking, "We have been here these four days, and You haven't shown up."

I could also see Martha running out to the Master. She was excited to see Him, but she held mixed emotions, as she said to Him, "If You had been here, my brother would not have died."

Many times we act that way. There are times when we give instructions, and the people go against our instruction. When they get into trouble, you know what we are always tempted to say? "I told you so." We are used to telling one another, "I told you so." Why do we do that? We do it to justify our correctness or our rightness. "I knew it all along that you were just going to miss it. I told you so!" Instead of acting the opposite, we actually make it hard for people to come to grips with what they are supposed to learn. Imagine if you came to the Lord and God told you, "I told you so." Do you know the guilt that would hit you? That guilt would keep you out of the house of God.

Martha was shifting the blame and putting it on Jesus, as ifHis delay killed her brother. That means the death of Lazarus had now become Jesus's responsibility. She said, "If you had been here, my brother would not have died. But I know that even now God will give you whatever you ask" (v. 22). But I know...but I know... That is the confident part. She *knew* that even now, whatever Jesus asked God, He will give it to Him.

DIVINE DELAY IS OFTEN A BLESSING IN DISGUISE.

Many times, God wants us to use this particular last part. No matter what has happened: It's been delayed, but I *know* that whatever You ask of God, He will still do it. It looks like I have been praying for thirty years. Had Jesus answered my prayer the first time I prayed, I wouldn't have gotten so deep in this problem. Always keep this in your heart— He is still the same yesterday, today, and forever. *But I know* that with God all things are possible. *But I know* that even though it's gone beyond normal time constraints, I have a God who can turn it around. *But I know* that the sickness has been around for fifteen or twenty years and is getting worse, but my God can heal it. *But I know* the financial situation is getting worse and worse. Even though I pray and fast, it's still getting worse and worse.

But I know that God can come through even in the eleventh

hour. It has been so difficult, and I wonder and even question if what I am doing is of the Lord, *but I know... but I know* my God will see me through, even though I accidentally find myself in the furnace of fire, and I see myself surrounded and pressed and pushed from every side, and it looks like I put myself in that situation. Therefore, I have to bring myself out. It is true that when *you* can't do it, there is One who can do it, and His name is Jesus.

When Jesus got close to Martha, He said, "Your brother will rise again" (v. 23).

Martha said, "I know he will rise again in the resurrection and at the last day" (v. 24).

Jesus said, "I am the resurrection. I am the last day. He will rise again because I am the beginning and the end. I am the resurrection. I am the essence of life."

She said, "Yes, Lord, I believe that you are the Christ, the Son of the living God, who was to come into this world."

After she had said this, she went back and called her sister, Mary, and said, "'The Teacher is here... and is asking for you.' When Mary heard this, she got up quickly and went to him. Now Jesus had not yet entered the village, but was still at the same place where Martha had met him. When the Jews who had been with Mary in the house, comforting her, noticed how quickly she got up and went out, they followed her, supposing she was going to the tomb to mourn there. When Mary reached the place where Jesus was and saw him, she fell at his feet and said, 'Lord, if you had been here, my brother would not have died'" (vv. 28–32). And when Jesus saw them weep, the Bible tells us that He also wept.

The interesting thing about this is that after four days, Lazarus was dead. He was stinking in the tomb, wrapped with burial clothes. His hands and feed were bound, and he could not breathe. After four days, Jesus Christ told them to remove the stone over the entrance to the tomb. He stood by the tomb and spoke to darkness as He called Lazarus. "Lazarus, come forth!" The Bible says that although Lazarus was dead, he heard His voice. This was past the time when observers expected anything to happen. On the first day, you might think that something could be done; but by this time, it had gone beyond the first day, beyond the second day, and beyond the third day. It is now the fourth day. Jesus said, "Lazarus, come forth!" The Bible says that the man who was dead heard His voice, rose, and came out.

The question is, why didn't Jesus go the moment He heard that Lazarus was sick? He was waiting for God to get the glory! The reason why God sometimes allows delays in answering our prayers is because *divine delay is a blessing in disguise!* God will always get glory in a situation that looks so far gone. Four days later, Lazarus was raised from the dead. He was a living testimony. He was a *delayed blessing.*

FROM BEGGING TO PRAISING

There is another incident in the Bible that comes to mind. According to Acts chapter 3, when Peter and John were getting close to the temple gate called Beautiful, they came across a crippled man who had been sitting by the same temple gate for many years, begging. On that day, he was looking for money. But Peter and John's response to him changed his attention from begging for alms to praising God.

In John 9 there is a story about a man who was born blind. The disciples asked Jesus: "Rabbi, who sinned, this man or his parents, that he was born blind?" (John 9:1). What did Jesus reply? He said, "Neither this man nor his parents sinned...but this happened so that the work of God might be displayed in his life" (v. 3).

Abraham and Sarah believed God to have children until they were past the age of bearing children. Then when Abraham was seventy-five years old, God gave him a promise. He said, "Abraham, you will have a son, and your wife is going to bear a son." (See Genesis 15:1–6.) If you received such a word, you would get excited, wouldn't you? You would immediately begin to work on it. You would shop for a crib and go to the bookstore to get a book on names. You would begin to exercise your muscles because you are going to be picking up a baby.

Abraham was seventy-five years old when God gave the promise, but it took another twenty-five years for that to happen. Abraham was ninety-nine years old when Sarah became pregnant. He was over one hundred when Isaac was born. Why did God delay? It was a *blessing in disguise*. God could have allowed the baby to come earlier, but Ishmael would have been a problem to that son. Remember that Abraham and Sarah had jumped ahead of God by arranging for Sarah's servant, Hagar, to birth Abraham's son Ishmael. Their impatience could have caused them to miss the promise of God for the generations to come. But God delayed the promise, and at the *appointed time* He allowed Isaac to be born.

Without a doubt, there will be times when you will pray and feel like God is not hearing. You will be tempted to wonder if your prayers are even reaching God, but never become discouraged. God is hearing you. You just don't know what He is doing behind the scenes. You cannot write the formula and say, "God is going to do this in two days, in three days." There are certain times when God will not do them as you expect so that your faith will not rest in what *you* say, but your faith will rest in what *He* says! The Word of God is more important than your word.

There are some prayers that I prayed many years ago. I would say there are some prayers that I prayed when I got saved—over thirty years ago—and I am just now beginning to see the answers to those prayers. God is beginning to remind me gradually of those prayers. At times God will remind you, "Remember what I did for you on this day and this day and this day." He will remind you that He wants you to celebrate Him and to praise your way out of every circumstance. *Divine delay is a blessing in disguise!*

Some of you have tried to knock some doors down, and God has had to tell you no, don't go through those doors. But everyone else may be telling you to go through that door, and so you push on that door with all your force, trying to force it open. You know you don't have strength enough, but you are determined. "I am going to open this door! I've been praying, and God doesn't seem to open the doors for me. Therefore, I am going to open my own doors." You are convinced that your persuasion in prayer has failed, and so you believe force must be applied. "I have been persuading God, and God seems to fail, so I am going to apply force—all by myself!"

GOD WORKS ACCORDING TO TIME AND SEASON, AND *HIS TIMING* IS OFTEN——IN FACT, *USUALLY*——DIFFERENT FROM OURS!

But when you cannot force the door open, you may become angry. By this time you have forgotten that God told you to wait, that He would show you the right door to open. Wait! *Divine delay is a blessing in disguise!* You always have to remember that God *will* come through! As people of God, we must always hold this confidence in our hearts: what God says, He is faithful to perform.

Scripture is given to us for an example—to teach, to edify, to encourage, and to uplift us. The biblical examples and stories that we have reviewed in this book have a direct application to us today. They are not given to us as mere chronicles of historical fact. As we review the circumstances under which God has answered His people over time, we come to see our daily lives in a different mind-set. We realize that God works according to *time and season,* and *His timing* is often—in fact, *usually*—different from ours!

When you are going through a difficult challenge, ask God

what He wants you to learn from the situation. How does God expect you to respond to these difficulties? Is God trying to teach you character, patience, perseverance, or perhaps working within *other* people who need to be involved to make your promises come to fruition? God is in control! He knows what He is doing and what it takes to fulfill the promise given you.

Careful review of biblical promises shows us that all of them took time. The Lord told Noah there would be a flood, but had it not *delayed*, Noah could not have built the ark. Joseph was given a dream that he would lead his family when he was yet a child. Joseph needed to go through many trials and testings to learn the wisdom that would be required of a prime minister of Egypt some seven-

ARMED WITH THIS KNOWLEDGE, YOU WILL REST CONFIDENT IN KNOWING THAT *DIVINE DELAY IS A BLESSING IN DISGUISE!*

teen years later and be in a position to save not only his family but also his nation from the perils of famine.

Even the birth of Jesus had a requirement of timing involved in it. We read in Galatians 4:4: "When the time had fully come, God sent his Son." Divine delay allowed our Savior to come into the world at the time appointed by God the Father when He had appropriately lined up all the events that needed to take place before His arrival.

In actuality, the Word tells us that God does everything "beautiful in its time" (Eccles. 3:11), which shows us that the aspect of delay, as we consider, is man's concept and not of God. God prepares the way for His plans to materialize in the most perfect and effectual way. Therefore, when we see *His* plan unfold, we see the awesome plan that only our God can put in place! Scripture goes on to tell us: "No eye has seen, no ear has heard, no mind has conceived what God has prepared for those who love him" (1 Cor. 2:9). When we recognize that God's ways are not our ways and that His wisdom exceeds ours, we become enlightened with patience to see the results that *He* has in store for us! Never allow anything or anyone to distract you from receiving God's best, or you will miss it.

Recognize that God's way is always the right way, though it may not appear evident at the moment. Understand that God proportions His people's trials to their strength.

> No temptation has seized you except what is common to man. And God is faithful; he will not let you be tempted beyond what you can bear. But when you are tempted, he will also provide a way out so that you can stand up under it.
>
> —1 CORINTHIANS 10:13

Finally, judge nothing before its time. Habakkuk 2:3 declares:

> For the revelation awaits an appointed time;
>   it speaks of the end
>   and will not prove false.
> Though it linger, wait for it;
>   it will certainly come and will not delay.

RISING ABOVE AVERAGE—THE MAKING OF A CHAMPION

T HE WORD *CHAMPION* IS a title that is used for those who have been through a struggle or battle and have come out on top. A champion is one who has been able to go against opposition and succeed. We tend to think of champions in the context of athletics— those who win sports titles, either individually or as part of a recognized team. It is not easy to become a champion.

Before developing into a champion, you need to study your subject and put in untold hours of commitment, training, exercise, and discipline. These principles also apply in many areas in which we can achieve championship beyond the sports arena.

God truly expects us all to be champions. It is interesting that we do not call Jesus Christ, who is really a champion, a champion; rather we call Him a *conqueror*. Yet, for us to assume the role of conquerors on Earth, we first have to become champions over the areas of our lives where responsibility has been placed. Jesus conquered the enemy for our benefit. We must conquer the challenges committed to our charge or sphere of influence.

The world does not perceive us as conquerors. When the world uses the term *conqueror*, it implies one who has been to battle where there has been a spilling of blood. In terms by which the world defines success, it sees only champions.

We need to understand the rules by which we will be able to become champions. Do you understand the importance of rising above average? Most people would respond that they do not wish to be average. In fact, most people would identify themselves as *above average*. Do you consider yourself above average? Be careful with making that declaration that you are not like many people whose egos have kicked in gear and caused them to think more highly of themselves than they ought!

Popular psychology declares that the enemy of excellence is *average*. There are two conditions that often lead to average: *apathy* and *mediocrity*. People who are apathetic or mediocre are people who are *satisfied* with life just as it is...just where they are. They may even say they are *fulfilled* or *content.* However, if you are going to be a *champion*, you're going to have to become a conqueror—a person who overcomes, lives outside the proverbial box, or goes beyond (above) average.

Average people give their best only when it's convenient for them to do so. But champions think like overcomers and believe that they have to conquer. Everything they do says, "I am not going to rest until I achieve the maximum goal or benefit."

I like the servant of God Moses as we see him in Exodus 33. Moses was not satisfied with his relationship with God, and he wanted *more.* He told God, "If you are pleased with me, teach me your ways so I may know you and continue to find favor with you" (Exod. 33:13). He was saying, "I don't want to stop here. I'm already favored, but I don't want the favor that I have to control the rest of my life. I want fresh favor every day."

THE MOMENT YOU BECOME SATISFIED, YOU BECOME RELIGIOUS.

Don't just settle for your last experience. The moment you become satisfied, you become religious. There is no zeal in you to go anymore. You do the same routine, day in and day out. You may actually perform your job responsibilities, but you no longer aim to achieve success or perfection in that job!

HAVE THE HEART OF A CHAMPION

You can always improve upon what you did in the past. An athlete who wants to be a champion trains hard. That person may desire to be a champion runner in track, but he understands that he will not just wake up one morning a champion—it will take months and years of preparation. He will diligently condition his mind, his spirit, and his soul. He goes to sleep at night and gets up in the morning with a passionate desire for victory. He constantly imagines himself already on the field in the starting gate, listening for the gunshot that says, "Go!" Everything in him is being conditioned and trained to be victorious over any previous track record. Once he breaks the record, even then he aims to improve upon his own record.

GOOD ENOUGH IS NOT GOOD ENOUGH FOR A CHAMPION!

When you refuse to improve, you become average. You become stale and unproductive, more like a lagoon than a river—in other words, nothing flows out of a stagnant body of water—no productivity, no success, no creativity!

Moses said (paraphrased), "Lord, if I have found favor with You, if You are pleased with me, and if You've been with me like You've said You've been with me, then teach me more ways. I don't want to settle for this; I don't want to be average. I want to pursue a relationship with You that is deeper than anything I have known."

You may have served well in your present position, but do it better today than you did yesterday. When your supervisor or mentor pressures you to do more, understand the benefit of pressure. Do you know that gold shines better when there is pressure on it? When you refuse to allow pressure to make you better, you are saying that your value should not attract the highest investor.

Life is too short to live your life as *average*. Be a champion— go for the gold! Always be improving and doing more today than you did in the past. A champion keeps on training…improving…rising to the next level. A champion never stops at *average. Good enough* is not good enough for a champion!

CONFRONT YOUR FEARS

It is also important to recognize that the thing you are afraid of is the very thing you have to confront. If you can confront it, you'll be free. You can't run away from your shadow; it depends upon how the light shines on it. Your shadow can either be in front of you, behind you, or beside you. It all depends on the angle of the light. The light of God will shine upon you, and you will see your own shadow. Don't run away from it, but rather confront it.

Confront your fears, confront your insecurities, confront your jealousies, confront the things that will take you off the course of success into failure. In order to progress in life, you have to confront whatever you are afraid of.

Fear of failure has kept many potentially successful and

prosperous people from achieving their goals. Success comes from avoiding unnecessary failure. At times, by taking calculated risks, we position ourselves to step into success. The ability to learn and grow from our early failures often teaches us the ability to recoup our losses and enhance our successes.

Albert Einstein once said, "Anyone who has never made a mistake has never tried anything new." Champions are those who are willing to step out and try!

IMPROVE UPON "GOOD"

In the Bible we learn that God is consistently seeking that which is "good." In Genesis 1:31 we read: "God saw all that he had made, and it was very good." It was what? It was "very good." James 1:17 tells us: "Every good and perfect gift is from above, coming down from the Father." Acts 10:38 says of Jesus, "He went around doing good and healing all who were under the power of the devil, because God was with him." Remember that anything done that is the opposite of good is not from God.

IT IS IMPORTANT TO RECOGNIZE THAT GOOD IS JUST THE STARTING POINT.

God wants us to improve upon good. He gave Adam and Eve authority over everything that had been created—the fields, the animals, everything in the sea. He gave it all to men. He said, "You cultivate it until it is perfected. Make something good out of it." (See Genesis 1:28–29.) God always likes making good out of something. He wants you and me to have the same attitude—a passion for making something good come out of that which He has given to our charge.

The Bible has identified God as the *Alpha* and the *Omega*: "I am Alpha and Omega, the beginning and the ending, saith the Lord" (Rev. 1:8, KJV). Whatever God begins, He finishes. We never attribute unfinished work to God, as unfinished work exhibits sloppiness. God would never quit something He had started, because whatever God starts is good. And because it's good, God wants to send blessing to it.

God will give you something good, but He wants you to improve upon what He has given you. God has given you gifts and talents. They are good in their initial form, but they become better when you add your God-given ability and improve them.

It is important to recognize that in the making of a champion, and in our quest to rise and live above average, good is just the starting point. Don't just settle with good. If you do, you will never strive to do anything better. There is something higher than good: it is called *better*. And there is something higher than better, which is called *best*. I like to phrase it this way: "When best is available, better is not good enough."

BE WILLING TO PAY THE PRICE

If you want what you see someone else has achieved, find out how much it costs to get it. Nothing comes to us for free! The reason why the Bible uses the word *free* is because believers like things free. God use the word *free* to get your attention, and when you get close, He says, "There's nothing free here." Whenever you think you find something for free, you have to ask, "What is the catch?" Anything costs, everything costs, anointing costs, blessings cost—everything you need is costly. It doesn't come cheap.

He has called you, but what price have you paid? You soon run out of gas if you've never paid the price. Rise above average and pay the right price so that nobody will contend with you for what you have achieved.

Was whatever you've been through worth it? At times you cry, and you may go through pain for a while, but when you begin to go through the victories, you will not even remember the pain. It's only when a woman is going through birth pains that she can feel the contractions, but once the baby is born, her cries are those of joy for the new life that has sprung forth. The good news is, something good has come into the world. God says, "I have the same thing for you. It's just positioned itself in the birth canal of opportunity, but you have to pay a price first to get it."

FOLLOW GODLY SUCCESS PRINCIPLES

When you learn certain basic success principles, they will take you wherever you need to go. You will advance wherever you go. I make friends based on principles. I am guided by principles wherever I go. I do the things that I do because of principles. I don't even try to do things that are not firmly rooted in godly principles. If principles are not related and I cannot benefit from them, I don't even try. Whatever is of great value has a price attached to it. Willingness to pay a price is also a principle that yields great dividends.

The process of rising above average can be a difficult and long one when we refuse to use the principles God teaches us. However, the sweetest victory comes when we claim the prize of championship in whatever area we strive to achieve. It is the satisfaction of a job well done. It is the victory of success over defeat. It means we have learned from principles and experience how to achieve above the norm. Charles Dickens wrote in *Little Dorrit*, "Every failure teaches a man something, if he will learn."[1] A vital lesson from this novel was that not all prisons have walls; often people build the chains that bind them with their own actions!

> LIFE IS TOO SHORT TO LIVE YOUR LIFE AS AVERAGE. BE A CHAMPION—GO FOR THE GOLD!

DO IT WITH EXCELLENCE

When we talk about success, we are not talking only about economic success. Success means being in charge of every area of your life. To be successful in all you are and all you do, you must do everything with excellence. Make excellence so much a part of you that it becomes your middle name. Choose what you want to do, and do it right—do it with excellence.

Have a desire to rise above average. Be a child of excellence. If you are a student, don't skip studying and still expect the

Holy Spirit to help you at exam time. The Bible says, "The Holy Spirit...will teach you all things, and bring to your remembrance all things" (John 14:26, NKJV). We also have the promise that "...my God shall supply all your need" (Phil. 4:19, NKJV). It is true that He will supply everything you need, but you must have planted a seed first. God supplies needs if He can see a seed. If a seed has been planted, He will turn it into supply of harvest.

Rising above average is an important principle to learn. It will require that you stop tolerating some of the things you have been tolerating. "Whatever you tolerate, you cannot change." God wants to prosper you. God wants to bless you. God wants to advance you. He doesn't want you to stay where you are. *God came to where we are to take us to where we need to be.* God doesn't want you to stay where you are. Please remember that anything in life that doesn't increase you will decrease you. Therefore, always strive to rise above the level where you find yourself.

Finish What You Start

In Genesis chapter 1, you can learn a great deal about God and His intentions. It reads:

> In the beginning God created the heavens and the earth. The earth was without form, and void; and darkness was on the face of the deep. And the Spirit of God was hovering over the face of the waters.
>
> —Genesis 1:1–2

According to many historians and Bible scholars, something significant occurred in between verses 1 and 2. The theory of a "gap" between Genesis 1:1 and 1:2 is referred to as the gap theory.[2] Many believe that it was between the time God first created the heavens and earth, when the earth was "without form, and void," that Lucifer was cast out of heaven. As a result of his fall, the earth became void, and God had to move upon the face of the waters and fix it again. That means God repaired the earth that had been destroyed by the fall of Lucifer and finished His creation efforts. Regardless of whether we ascribe to the gap theory, we can recognize that between these two verses there was time and opportunity.

> THE SWEETEST VICTORY COMES WHEN WE CLAIM THE PRIZE OF CHAMPIONSHIP IN WHATEVER AREA WE STRIVE TO ACHIEVE.

To become a true champion, never stop looking for new results. Refuse to dwell on past accomplishments. Yesterday is gone, and today is a new day. Endeavor to approach each new day with new enthusiasm to perform every task to the maximum benefit.

Champions are people who walk in excellence. Their focus is not upon the things they are going through; their focus is on where they are going. Where are you going? Show me where you are going, and I can help direct you on the path to get there. If you don't know where you are going, any path you take would only lead you to nowhere!

Champions are always looking ahead. Don't do anything with only half your effort, because it will catch up with you in the future. Whatever you do, do it with excellence. Excellence will qualify you for promotion. You can actually become unnecessary in your present assignment and be promoted to something new and more substantial than anything you have done in the past.

The making of a champion is often the process of stepping beyond average, of moving above failure, of taking the good we are presented with as stepping-stones, and creating a new history where we are the victors! This ability rests within each of us. We need only to tap into it and rise above average!

13

TAKE A LOOK AT ME NOW!

WHEN YOU LOOK AT what you have accomplished in life, if you are not saved or grounded in God, you will think you did it by your own strength. There are also certain times when, if you are also not grounded in God, you will blame everyone else for what has not happened in your life. One of the challenges we face is the process of finding the *balance*. Our strength comes from the Lord, our wisdom comes from the Lord; but *He* expects *us* to utilize the gifts and talents He has planted within us. As we discussed earlier, there is a *process* involved wherein we are seasoned and trained by the circumstances He places in our path. There is a price to be paid, and until we have walked out the course He has designed for us, we will not see the victory.

I learned early in life that I didn't want anything for free. I wanted to pay a price for everything. If you don't learn this lesson as a teenager, you will be a mess when you grow up. A woman who marries a man who doesn't like to work is marrying trouble. A woman who marries a man who runs to his mother and father all the time for money has married trouble. Parents, don't spoil your children! Women, don't try to spoil your husbands! Push your husbands out of the bed and get them to work. If they don't work, your grandchildren will curse you. We must teach our children to start early. When you start working early, your dreams get bigger. People who don't work, don't dream—they fantasize.

You have to pay a price in order to become what God wants you to be, but if your children can never remember what they've been through—no spanking, no discipline, and all they remember is you putting everything in their hands—your children will never be able to dream. They will only fantasize and never capture the right dream.

I look at myself and the course God has taken my life. Even though there may have been times the voice of God was dim, I am still here! I am still serving God, and my life is full. God hasn't forgotten me, and He has great plans for me. *Take a look at me now!* Years ago, no one would have predicted the areas of responsibility that would rest in my hands. This would not have been possible without the Lord, but *He* knew the plans He had for me, and He directed my path!

Take a look at *you* now! Just take a look at you. I'm not tellingyou to take a look at the picture the enemy wants to paint! I'm saying, take a look at you now. If you can see yourself through the mirror of time, or through the eyes of God, you will see what God intends for your life.

Yes, take a good look at you! Say, "Life is worth living if you live it in Jesus Christ." You can say with pride, *take a look at me now!*

IF YOU CAN SEE YOURSELF THROUGH THE MIRROR OF TIME, OR THROUGH THE EYES OF GOD, YOU WILL SEE WHAT GOD INTENDS FOR YOUR LIFE.

"For our light and momentary troubles are achieving for us an eternal glory that far outweighs them all" (2 Cor. 4:17). So, what are we supposed to do? Verse 18 tells us: "So we fix our eyes not on what is seen, but on what is unseen. For what is seen is temporary, but what is unseen is eternal."

Job understood this principle while he was going through his pain. I could hear Job say to his friends, "Just open your eyes, and take a look at me. You knew me to be a man of substance, but what I'm going through is temporal, because what I had needed to be multiplied, and after I go through this process, my abundance will come. Let me go through this."

When his wife came and said, "Man, curse God and die," he said, "What a foolish woman." When his friends mocked him and laughed at him, it didn't faze him. He said, "Lord, even though You slay me, yet will I serve You" (see Job 13:15), because deep in his heart he knew himself, and he *saw* himself. He was able to assert to them: "Take a good look at me; what I'm going through is not the real picture."

WORKING FOR GOD'S DREAM IN YOU

Joseph is a key example of a dreamer in Scripture, as we read in Genesis 37. Joseph was seventeen years old when he started having dreams, and the dream was so important that it attracted problems for him. The Bible says in verse 5, "Joseph had a dream, and when he told it to his brothers, they hated him all the more." *They hated him because he was loved.*

The Bible goes on to tell us in verse 9 that he had another dream. This time in his dream the sun and the moon and eleven stars were bowing down to him. When he told his father about this dream, he received his father's rebuke. There are certain times you need a rebuke to keep you holding the dream and not spilling it. Holding your dream can actually become sacred. At times it is more important to hold your dream within your heart—until God's appointed time—than to pour it out before those who could destroy or kill you with it.

Jesus did the same thing with the disciples. When He trained them, He sent them out to go minister. When they came back, they were excited about the miracles. He said to them, "That's good, but be happy that your names are written in heaven." (See Luke 10:20.) He was waiting for the right time for them to be released. He wanted them to dream, but He knew that they would have to work for their dreams. When you work for a dream, no man can claim they made you. Even though God will use people to shape and mold you into the kind of person you were supposed to become, God is the One who is to be praised.

> AT TIMES IT IS MORE IMPORTANT TO HOLD YOUR DREAM WITHIN YOUR HEART——UNTIL GOD'S APPOINTED TIME——THAN TO POUR IT OUT BEFORE THOSE WHO COULD DESTROY OR KILL YOU WITH IT.

Joseph started running into problems when he began telling others about his dreams. His brothers not only hated him, but they also were very jealous of him. His brothers became so jealous of him that they sold him into slavery. He ended up in Egypt.

> Now Joseph had been taken down to Egypt. Potiphar, an Egyptian who was one of Pharaoh's officials, the captain of the guard, bought him from the Ishmaelites who had taken him there.
>
> —GENESIS 39:1

The Bible tells us:

> The LORD was with Joseph and he prospered, and he
> lived in the house of his Egyptian master. When his
> master saw that the LORD was with him and that the
> LORD gave him success in everything he did, Joseph
> found favor in his eyes and became his attendant.
> Potiphar put him in charge of his household, and he
> entrusted to his care everything he owned.
> —GENESIS 39:2–4

How can a slave prosper? The Lord gave him success in everything he did. That means if you find favor, you will serve the right people. Serving is a sign of favor. If you serve the Lord, it means you found the favor of God. If you're serving somebody who can bless you, that means you found the favor of God. But if you're not serving anybody, it's a sign that there is no favor in your life.

The Bible tells us that Potiphar put him in charge of all his household. The Lord blessed the household of an Egyptian because of Joseph. He prospered the Egyptian home, even though in Egypt they worship idols. "The blessing of the LORD was on everything Potiphar had, both in the house and in the field. So he left in Joseph's care everything he had; with Joseph in charge, he did not concern himself with anything except the food he ate" (vv. 5–6).

If you serve well, your countenance will make you look beautiful or handsome. But if you don't serve anybody, you will always be down and depressed. When you serve God with gladness, or you serve your boss with gladness, whomever you serve, serve faithfully. People will see you later on and say, "Is this really the person we saw serving? She looks like Esther to me...she looks like Ruth to me...he looks like Mordecai to me. Is that the same person?"

Often your body language is a sign of what is happening inside you. So, if you really want to serve God with gladness and be blessed, change your heart. With some people you can tell by their attitude that it doesn't benefit them to serve and that they will never do anything significant for God.

> IF YOU SERVE WELL, YOUR COUNTENANCE WILL MAKE YOU LOOK BEAUTIFUL OR HANDSOME.

But as we look at Joseph, we see that everything he did prospered. They gave them authority. You can't keep a dreamer down; a dreamer will always have the dreams. He may have been in prison, but the dream was still in him. You can't stop a dreamer because they will serve their way to the top!

God has some things in store for you, and He wants you to come to the top. He wants you to hold on to the dream, but more than that, God wants you to be a servant.

Ultimately, Joseph got the king's attention. Pharaoh had a dream he could not interpret. Word came to him: "Hey, there's a young Hebrew guy here who can interpret all these dreams. May we call him in and ask of him the meaning of the dream?"

Pharaoh found out that Joseph had the ability to interpret dreams.

In Genesis 41:38–40 we read:

> So Pharaoh asked them, "Can we find anyone like this man, one in whom is the spirit of God?" Then Pharaoh said to Joseph, "Since God has made all this known to you, there is no one so discerning and wise as you. You shall be in charge of my palace."

Can you see that? From the time he left prison, everywhere he went he encountered promotion. He would not have been promoted if he had not gotten into trouble and learned to serve his captors.

Take a look at him now! Had his brothers loved him when he had the dream, showing love instead of jealousy because he was his father's favorite, and not sold him, he would have blended in with the crowd and actually been removed from the preparation of the works of God in his life. Remember that divine delay is a blessing in disguise! For Joseph, it placed him in the position God had ordained for him, where he could become a blessing not only to his family but also to an entire nation. *Take a look at him now!*

Joseph knew God. He had a relationship with God, and in spite of what he was going through, his ability to interpret dreams demonstrated his wisdom. Pharaoh's magicians and wise men could not give him the meaning to his dream, but this little Hebrew boy who came with a dream of his own was eventually promoted because of the favor of God. It does not matter where you start in life—what is important is to realize that the place where you end up is your place of destiny!

What price have you paid for your dream? "We do not want you to become lazy, but to imitate those who through faith and patience inherit what has been promised" (Heb. 6:12). In Matthew 7:20 we discover: "Thus, by their fruit you will recognize them."

I am not saying, "Show me your eloquence or your intelligence." I am asking you, "What fruits do you have?" Look at me now; look at you now; look at what God is going to do in your life. Many of you had families who thought you were crazy when you started going to church. They could not understand the power of your dream. They thought you would never see success. *But look at you now!*

Look with me at 2 Corinthians 4:8: "We are hard pressed on every side, but not crushed." We have all experienced some pressures in our lives from time to time. Many of you reading this book may be experiencing those pressures right now. I'm talking about pressures in all areas of your life—spiritual pressure, financial pressure, marital pressure, business pressure, decisions you have to make about which you are not very clear. The Bible tells us that this is not new; it's bound to happen. But remember this:

> THE MOMENT YOU CONCEDE THAT THE BEST OF THE YEARS ARE PAST, YOU HAVE CONCLUDED FAILURE AS YOUR PORTION.

you are pressed, hard pressed, not softly or gently, but the good news here is that you are not crushed. In spite of your perplexities you are not in despair. You are persecuted, but you are not abandoned. God will not allow you to be destroyed. He will not let that happen even though you may be struck down. The Word tells us that "for though a righteous man falls seven times, he rises again, but the wicked are brought down by calamity" (Prov. 24:16). That means that when the righteous fall, God will pick them up.

When God is at work in your life, He may squeeze things out of you in order to put some things in you. God has to squeeze out the negatives, some unbelief, some fears, and some failures. When you are going through challenges and feel squeezed, don't look for someone to blame! Who told you that everything would be solved on time? Who said that you would take the fast track to success? Did GOD say it? Or did those around you try to convince you that the only way is the easy way?

EXPECT GOD'S QUESTIONING

Have you ever noticed that when God asks questions, it is a serious matter? Just think about it: God actually asks man questions, and He expects good answers!

Let's take a look at some of the first questions God asked of man. In Genesis chapter 3, God came across Adam and Eve in the garden, just after they had just been deceived by Satan.

In Genesis 3:9–11 we read the following:

> But the LORD God called to the man, "Where are you?" He answered, "I heard you in the garden, and I was afraid because I was naked; so I hid." And he said, "*Who told you* that you were naked? Have you eaten from the tree that I commanded you not to eat from?"
>
> —EMPHASIS ADDED

While we recognize that it was their conscience that told them they were naked, the actions that precipitated this were as a result of them listening to the lies of Satan.

I find it very interesting that from the very first struggle that man encountered, Satan was already at work deceiving man and *telling them something different than what God said*! And...they believed it! What we need to understand here is that if *God* didn't say it, then it is just someone else's opinion! God is in charge! He is the author and the finisher—yes, of our faith—but of *all* things. He *knows* the beginning from the end. He has measured our days before there was even one of them. And if *God* didn't say it, then it isn't so!

> GOD MAY SQUEEZE THINGS OUT OF YOU IN ORDER TO PUT SOME THINGS IN YOU.

God's third question is also very telling to us: "What is this you have done?" (v. 13). In other words, what business do you have listening to the opinions of others? God is revealing something significant to us here if we will only listen! God is giving us confirmation that *His* Word is the final word! *He* is the One who has the authority to speak into our lives and direct them. *He* has only good in store for us! We are told in Jeremiah 29:11, "'For I know the plans I have for you,' declares the LORD, 'plans to prosper you and not to harm you, plans to give you hope and a future.'"

It is time we stopped believing the lies of the enemy! Break free from your limitations, renew your mind, and become all that you are destined to be! God has placed within you unlimited potential. The only limitation is the one you place upon yourself. *Who says you can't?* Perhaps *you* are the very one saying it!

Jesus said that all authority in heaven and Earth has been given to Him, and He, in turn, has given it to us through His Word. We have the confidence He has given us, but we have to renew *our* minds to accept it and walk in it!

There is a glory that is about to be revealed that far outweighs what you've been through. That means your troubles were worth it! The value of your glory is demonstrated in your struggles; the price you are paying is worth it. Let me remind you: never come to the point in your life when you conclude that *the worst is yet to come.* No matter what you go through, God always reminds us in His Word that *the best is yet to come!* God still has great plans for your life, no matter what you may go through! The moment you concede that the best of the years are past, you have concluded failure as your portion. Remind yourself that "even though I walk through the valley of the shadow of

LIFE IS WORTH LIVING IF YOU LIVE IT IN JESUS CHRIST.

death, I will fear no evil, for you are with me" (Ps. 23:4). Remind yourself of what God has done for you. It may have been difficult, but God has always seen us through.

God does not deal with opinions; opinions are hypothetical. God deals with truth. And what you think shall be what you become. The Bible says that as a man "thinketh in his heart, so is he" (Prov. 23:7, KJV). So you have to be careful what you're thinking. Thinking is the processing of the materials you put in. When you look at yourself, what do you think? If your thinking is not right, everything around you will be wrong. You have to think right.

What is your thinking? Negative thinking, doubtful thinking, unbelieving thinking—whatever you think is a process of the materials collected. The Bible tells us that the person who is double minded is unstable. A person becomes whatever that person is constantly thinking. That means that when you are processing the wrong material—thoughts, emotions, reflections—those wrong materials will become who you are.

Therefore, my meditation has become the Word of the Lord. What God says is more important to me than what's happening around me. Do you believe what God says? Think about this:

> Finally, brothers, whatever is true, whatever is noble, whatever is right, whatever is pure, whatever is lovely, whatever is admirable—if anything is excellent or praiseworthy—think about such things.
>
> —Philippians 4:8

If you're going to think, think the way God wants you to think. Process things the way God wants you to process things.

Don't let your mind become a garbage center, a recycling center.

WHAT YOU THINK
SHALL BE WHAT YOU
BECOME

You have to set your mind free. You have to *renew your mind*:

Do not conform any longer to the pattern of this world, but be transformed by the renewing of your mind. Then you will be able to test and approve what God's will is—his good, pleasing and perfect will.

—ROMANS 12:2

It is what God says that is important!

He asked the first Adam, "Who told you...?" He also asks us, "Who says you can't?" Did God say it? If He said it, then it is truth; but if you are listening to someone else, you may be setting yourself up for failure!

- *Who says you can't...* finish that degree?

- *Who says you can't...* land that successful job?

- *Who says you can't...* own your own home?

- *Who says you can't...* have a family?

- *Who says you can't...* patent your invention?

- *Who says you can't*...run your own company?

- *Who says you can't*...run for political office?

- *Who says you can't*...impact the lives of multitudes?

- *Who says you can't*...dream your dreams and bring all of them into reality?

NOTES

CHAPTER 1
WHO SAYS YOU CAN'T?

1. Napoleon Hill, *Think and Grow Rich* (San Diego, CA: Aventine Press, 2004).

2. Simon Sebag Montefiore, *Speeches That Changed the World* (Australia: Murdoch Books, 2007).

3. For more about the life of Mahatma Ghandi, see "Gandhi, Mohandas Karamchand," Microsoft (R) Encarta. Copyright © 1993 Microsoft Corporation. Copyright © 1993 Funk & Wagnall's Corporation.

4. About.com: Women's History, "Princess Diana's Wedding," http:// womenshistory.about.com/od/diana/a/diana_wedding.htm (accessed September 12, 2008).

5. For more about the life of Princess Diana, see Andrew Morton, *Diana: Her True Story—in Her Own Words* (London: Michael O'Mara Books, 2003).

CHAPTER 2
FEAR EQUALS FAILURE

1. ThinkExist.com, "Franklin D. Roosevelt Quotes," http://thinkexist .com/quotation/there_is_nothing_to_fear_but_fear_itself/205789 .html (accessed September 11, 2008).

2. Jack Canfield and Mark Victor Hansen, *Chicken Soup for the Soul* (Deerfield Beach, FL: Health Communications, 1993), 236–37.

3. Ibid., 236.

4. The Quotations Page, "Albert Einstein Quotes," http://www .quotationspage.com/quote/26032.html (accessed September 11, 2008).

5. For more information about Ronald Reagan, visit the Ronald Reagan Presidential Foundation & Library at http://www.reagan library.com/reagan/biography/.

CHAPTER 3
BREAKING THE CHAINS OF STIGMA

1. Les Brown, *It's Not Over Until You Win* (New York: Simon & Schuster, 1998), 141–172.

2. Ibid.

CHAPTER 5
WHO SAYS YOU CAN?

1. "Colin Powell Quotes," http://www.people.ubr.com/political/by-first-name/c/colin-powell/colin-powell-quotes.aspx (accessed July 15, 2008).

2. Myles, Munroe, *Releasing Your Potential* (Shippensburg, PA: Destiny Image, 1996), Preface. Materials from *Releasing Your Potential*, by Myles Munroe, copyright © 1992, used by permission of Destiny Image Publishers, 167 Walnut Bottom Road, Shippensburg, PA 17257. www.destinyimage.com.

3. Robert Schuller, *Tough Times Never Last, But Tough People Do!* (New York: Bantam Books, 1984), 125–142.

CHAPTER 6
PURPOSE, PLAN, AND PROCESS

1. Munroe, *Releasing Your Potential*, 199–202. Used by permission.

2. One version of this Native American tale can be see at BrightQuotes.com, "Native American," at http://brightquotes.com/na_fr.html (accessed July 15, 2008).

3. Les Brown, *It's Not Over Until You Win*, 141–172.

4. "Sheila Johnson: America's First Black Female Billionaire—Biography," http://findarticles.com/p/articles/mi_m1077/is_11_58/ai_106700553 (accessed September 15, 2008).

5. For more information about Oprah Winfrey, see http://www.oprah.com/about (accessed July 15, 2008).

CHAPTER 7
OVERCOMING THE ODDS

1. Helen Keller, *The Story of My Life* (New York: W.W. Norton & Co., 2003).

2. Notable Biographies, "Helen Keller Biography," http://www.notable biographies.com/Jo-Ki/Keller-Helen.html (accessed July 17, 2008).

3. Morehouse College, "Morehouse Legacy," http://www.morehouse .edu/about/legacy.html (accessed September 15, 2008).

4. Answers.com, "Biography: Johnnetta Cole," http://www.answers .com/topic/johnnetta-b-cole-1 (accessed September 16, 2008).

5. JesseOwens.com, "Biography," http://www.jesseowens.com/ biography/ (accessed September 16, 2008).

CHAPTER 9
TRAGEDY AND TRIUMPH

1. Charles Lindbergh, *"We"* (Guilford, CT: The Lyons Press, 1927, 2002).

2. CharlesLindbergh.com, "Charles Lindbergh Biography," http:// www.charleslindbergh.com/history/index.asp (accessed September 16, 2008).

3. Mothers Against Drunk Driving, "About Us," http://www.madd .org/About-Us.aspx (accessed September 16, 2008).

4. Ibid.

5. For more information about Lance Armstrong, visit www .lancearmstrong.com.

6. United Farm Workers, "The Story of Cesar Chavez: The Beginning," http://www.ufw.org/_page.php?menu=research&inc=history/07.html (accessed September 16, 2008).

7. The Official Site of the Presidential Medal of Freedom, "Medal of Freedom," http://www.medaloffreedom.com/CesarChavez.htm (accessed September 16, 2008).

8. Tanisha Bagley, *The Price of Love* (New Bern, NC: Trafford, 2004).

9. Ibid.

10. Ibid.

11. Ibid.

12. For more information about this documentary film, see http://www
.wral.com/news/local/story/110464/ (accessed July 18, 2008).

Chapter 12
Rising Above Average—
the Making of a Champion

1. Charles Dickens, *Little Dorrit* (New York : Penguin Books, 1868, 1998), 390.

2. For more information regarding the gap theory, see Bert Thompson, PhD, "Popular Compromises of Creation—the Gap Theory," *Apologetics Press.org*, at http://www.apologeticspress.org/articles/442 (accessed July 25, 2008).